...ed by a new sense of freedom' *The Independent*

'A different approach. A stunning success' *The Sun*

'His skill is in removing the psychological dependence'
Sunday Times

'Allow Allen Carr to help you escape today' *The Observer*

'Allen Carr explodes the myth that giving up smoking is
difficult' *The Times*

'The smoker does not feel he is depriving himself by stopping'
The Guardian

'I suffered no serious withdrawal pangs . . . a month later I still
have no desire to smoke' *The Daily Telegraph*

'Afterwards I couldn't believe that I didn't want to smoke – but
I didn't . . . after five months I haven't had a single cigarette!'
Sunday Express

'An intelligent and original method' *London Evening Standard*

'For the first time in my adult life I am free' *Woman's Journal*

'I always thought if I didn't have the strength to stop on my own
– how could anyone else help – I can honestly say 4 months later
– I haven't missed cigarettes at all' *Zest*

'I've never been more confident about not smoking' *Tatler*

'In the pub I couldn't understand why I didn't want a cigarette –
but I didn't. Weird! Six months later and I haven't touched a
cigarette' *Front*

'I reckon this method is as close to fool proof as it gets, so don't bank on having to get your refund under the money back guarantee' *Time Out*

'The Allen Carr method is totally unique in its approach to stopping smoking. We are convinced that this is the way forward for a non-smoking future' *GQ Magazine*

'If you are one of those folk single-handedly keeping your local tobacconist in business, but want to ditch the demon weed, this is for you' *OK! Magazine*

What established professionals and medical practitioners say about the Allen Carr method:

'I have no hesitation in supporting Allen Carr's work in helping smokers quit. Many quitting clinics use some of his techniques, but it would appear few do so in quite such a successful package.' *A personal view from Professor Judith Mackay, MBE, Director, Asian Consultancy on Tobacco Control and World Health Organisation Expert, Advisory Panel on Tobacco and Health*

'It is a remarkable fact that Allen Carr, on his own admission a nonprofessional in behaviour modification, should have succeeded where countless psychologists and psychiatrists holding postgraduate qualifications have failed, in formulating a SIMPLE and EFFECTIVE way to stop smoking.' *Dr William Green, Head of the Psychiatric Department, Matilda Hospital, Hong Kong*

'I was really impressed by the method. In spite of Allen Carr's success and fame, there were no gimmicks and the professional approach was something a GP could readily respect. I would be happy to give a medical endorsement of the method to anyone.' *Dr P. M. Bray*

'I have observed the Allen Carr method, "The Easy Way to Stop Smoking", at first hand on several occasions. I have found it to be very successful. I wholeheartedly support it as an effective way to stop smoking.' *Dr Anil Visram, B.Sc., MBBch, FRCA, Consultant, The Royal Hospitals NHS Trust, Royal London Hospital, UK*

The common thread running through Allen Carr's work is the removal of fear. Indeed, his genius lies in eliminating the phobias and anxieties which prevent people from being able to enjoy life to the full, as his bestselling books *Allen Carr's Easy Way to Stop Smoking*, *The Only Way to Stop Smoking Permanently*, *Allen Carr's Easyweigh to Lose Weight*, *Allen Carr's Easyway To Control Alcohol*, *How to Stop Your Child Smoking*, and *The Easy Way to Enjoy Flying*, vividly demonstrate.

A successful accountant, Allen Carr's hundred-cigarettes-a-day addiction was driving him to despair until, in 1983, after countless failed attempts to quit, he finally discovered what the world had been waiting for: an Easy Way to Stop Smoking. Together with Robin Hayley, whom he appointed as Managing Director of Allen Carr's Easyway Worldwide, he went on to build a network of clinics that span the globe and have a phenomenal reputation for success in helping smokers to quit and a global publishing programme. His books have been published in over thirty-six different languages in over fifty different countries and DVD, audio, CD-ROM, video game and webcast versions of his method are also available. Allen also nominated Robin as his successor and gave him responsibility for his lasting legacy.

Hundreds of thousands of people have attended Allen Carr's Easyway clinics where, with a success rate of over 90 per cent, they guarantee that you will find it easy to quit smoking or your money back. A full list of clinics appears in the back of this book. Should you require any assistance do not hesitate to contact your nearest clinic.

Weight-control and alcohol sessions are now offered at a selection of these clinics. A full corporate service is also available enabling companies to implement stop smoking programmes in the workplace simply and effectively.

All correspondence and enquiries about Allen Carr's EASY-WAY books, DVDs, audios, CD-ROMs, video games and webcasts should be addressed to the London Head Office and Clinic listed at the back of this book.

Allen Carr's Easy Way to Stop Smoking

Be a happy non-smoker for the rest of your life

Fourth Edition

PENGUIN BOOKS

PENGUIN BOOKS

Published by the Penguin Group
Penguin Books Ltd, 80 Strand, London WC2R ORL, England
Penguin Group (USA) Inc., 375 Hudson Street, New York, New York 10014, USA
Penguin Group (Canada), 90 Eglinton Avenue East, Suite 700, Toronto, Ontario, Canada M4P 2Y3
(a division of Pearson Penguin Canada Inc.)
Penguin Ireland, 25 St Stephen's Green, Dublin 2, Ireland
(a division of Penguin Books Ltd)
Penguin Group (Australia), 250 Camberwell Road, Camberwell, Victoria 3124, Australia
(a division of Pearson Australia Group Pty Ltd)
Penguin Books India Pvt Ltd, 11 Community Centre, Panchsheel Park, New Delhi – 110 017, India
Penguin Group (NZ), 67 Apollo Drive, Rosedale, North Shore 0632, New Zealand
(a division of Pearson New Zealand Ltd)
Penguin Books (South Africa) (Pty) Ltd, 24 Sturdee Avenue, Rosebank, Johannesburg 2196, South Africa

Penguin Books Ltd, Registered Offices: 80 Strand, London WC2R ORL, England

www.penguin.com

First published privately, under the title *The Easy Way to Stop Smoking*, by Allen Carr 1985
Published in Penguin Books 1987
Second edition 1991
Third edition 1999
Reissued with a new introduction 2004
Fourth edition 2009
008

Copyright © Allen Carr's Easyway (International) Limited, 1985, 1991, 1999, 2004, 2006, 2009

Set in 12.5/14.75 pt Monotype Fournier
Typeset by Rowland Phototypesetting Ltd, Bury St Edmunds, Suffolk
Printed in England by Clays Ltd, St Ives plc

ISBN: 978–0–141–03940–4

www.greenpenguin.co.uk

Penguin Books is committed to a sustainable
future for our business, our readers and our planet.
This book is made from Forest Stewardship
Council™ certified paper.

MIX
Paper from
responsible sources
FSC® C018179

ALWAYS LEARNING

PEARSON

To the smokers I have failed to cure,
I hope it will help them to get free

Also to Sid Sutton

But most of all to Joyce

Contents

Preface

Just suppose there were a magic method of stopping smoking which enables any smoker, *including you*, to quit:

- IMMEDIATELY
- PERMANENTLY
- WITHOUT NEEDING WILLPOWER
- WITHOUT SUFFERING WITHDRAWAL SYMPTOMS
- WITHOUT PUTTING ON WEIGHT
- WITHOUT SHOCK TACTICS, PILLS, PATCHES OR OTHER GIMMICKS

Let's further suppose that:

- THERE IS NO INITIAL PERIOD OF FEELING DEPRIVED OR MISERABLE
- YOU IMMEDIATELY ENJOY SOCIAL OCCASIONS MORE
- YOU FEEL MORE CONFIDENT AND BETTER EQUIPPED TO HANDLE STRESS
- YOU ARE BETTER ABLE TO CONCENTRATE

- YOU DON'T SPEND THE REST OF YOUR LIFE HAVING TO RESIST THE OCCASIONAL TEMPTATION TO LIGHT A CIGARETTE

and

- YOU NOT ONLY FIND IT EASY TO QUIT, BUT CAN ACTUALLY ENJOY THE PROCESS FROM THE MOMENT YOU EXTINGUISH THE LAST CIGARETTE

If there were such a magical method, would you use it?

Chances are you would. But of course you don't believe in magic. Neither do I. Nevertheless the method I describe above does exist. I call it EASYWAY. In fact it isn't magic, it just seems that way. It certainly seemed that way to me when I first discovered it and I know that many of the millions of ex-smokers who have successfully quit with the help of EASYWAY also view it in that light.

No doubt you still find my claims difficult to believe. Don't worry, I would regard you as somewhat naive if you just accepted them without proof. On the other hand do not make the mistake of dismissing them because you believe they are grossly exaggerated. In all probability you are only reading this book because of the recommendation of an ex-smoker who attended an Allen Carr's EASYWAY clinic, read this book or stopped by using another Allen Carr product. It doesn't matter whether you received the recommendation directly or via someone who loves you and is desperately worried that unless you quit, you won't be there to go on loving.

How does EASYWAY work? That is not easy to describe

briefly. Smokers arrive at our clinics in differing states of panic, convinced that they won't succeed and believing that even if by some miracle they do manage to quit, they will first have to endure an indeterminable period of abject misery, that social occasions will never be quite so enjoyable, that they will be less able to concentrate and cope with stress and that, although they might never smoke again, they will never be completely free and that for the rest of their lives they will have occasional yearnings to smoke a cigarette and will have to resist the temptation.

The majority of those smokers leave the clinics a few hours later already happy non-smokers. How do we achieve that miracle? You need to book an appointment at an Allen Carr's EASYWAY clinic to find out. However, what I can say is that most smokers expect us to achieve that objective by telling them of the terrible health risks that they run, that smoking is a filthy disgusting habit, that it costs them a fortune, and how stupid they are not to quit. No. We do not patronize them by telling them what they already know. These are the problems of being a smoker. They are not the problems of quitting. Smokers do not smoke for the reasons that they shouldn't smoke. In order to quit it is necessary to remove the reasons that we do smoke. EASYWAY addresses this problem. It removes the desire to smoke. Once the desire to smoke has been removed, the ex-smoker doesn't need to use willpower.

The EASYWAY method exists in the form of clinics, books, DVDs, audios, CD-ROMs, video games and webcasts. In each case the method is the same, they are merely different vehicles to communicate it. Which vehicle should you use? It's a question of personal choice. Some people prefer reading books, others prefer watching DVDs. The clinics enjoy such a high success rate that we are able to give a money-back guarantee. The fee varies according to location and if you are one of the 20 per cent who requires more than one visit, you can attend any number of follow-ups without further charge. We never give up on any smoker. And if you fail to stop smoking once the programme is completed, your fee will be refunded in full. On the basis of our money-back guarantee, the worldwide success rate at our clinics averages over 90 per cent.

Do not let any of the above detract from the value of this book. It is a complete course in itself and millions of smokers have quit easily simply by reading it. If you are in doubt, why not telephone your nearest clinic for further guidance. A list of clinics appears at the back of the book.

Warning

Perhaps you are somewhat apprehensive about reading this book. Perhaps, like the majority of smokers, the mere thought of stopping fills you with panic and although you have every intention of stopping one day, it is not today.

If you are expecting me to inform you of the terrible health risks that smokers run, that smokers spend a small fortune during their smoking lives, that it is a filthy, disgusting habit and that you are a stupid, spineless, weak-willed jellyfish, then I must disappoint you. Those tactics never helped me to quit and if they were going to help you, you would already have quit.

My method, which I shall refer to as EASYWAY, doesn't work that way. Some of the things that I am about to say, you might find difficult to believe. However by the time you've finished the book, you'll not only believe them, but wonder how you could ever have been brainwashed to believe otherwise.

There is a common misapprehension that we choose to smoke. Smokers no more choose to smoke than drinkers choose to become alcoholics, or heroin takers choose to become junkies. It is true that we choose to light those first experimental cigarettes. I occasionally choose to go to the cinema, but I certainly wouldn't choose to spend my whole life there.

Please reflect on your life. Did you ever make the positive decision that you wouldn't be able to enjoy a meal or a social occasion without smoking, or that you wouldn't be able to concentrate or handle stress without a cigarette? At what stage did you decide that you needed cigarettes, not just for social occasions, but that you needed to have them permanently with you, and felt insecure, even panic stricken, without them?

Like every other smoker, you have been lured into the most sinister and subtle trap that man and nature have combined to devise. There is not a parent on this planet, whether they be smoker or non-smoker, that likes the thought of their children smoking. This means that all smokers wish they had never started. Not surprising really, no one needs cigarettes to enjoy meals or cope with stress before they get hooked.

At the same time all smokers wish to continue to smoke. After all, no one forces us to light up and, whether they understand the reason or not, it's only smokers themselves who decide to light up.

If there were a magic button that smokers could press to wake up the following morning as if they had never lit that first cigarette, the only smokers there would be tomorrow morning would be the youngsters who are still at the experimental stage. The only thing that prevents us from quitting is: FEAR!

Fear that we will have to survive an indeterminate period of misery, deprivation and unsatisfied craving in order to be free; fear that a meal or social occasion will never be quite as enjoyable without a cigarette; fear that we'll never be able to concentrate, handle stress or be as confident without our little crutch; fear that our personality or character will change; but most of all, the fear that 'once a smoker, always a smoker', that we will never be completely free and spend the rest of our lives at odd times craving the occasional cigarette. If, as I did, you have already tried all the conventional ways to quit and been through the misery of what I describe as the Willpower Method of stopping, you will be profoundly influenced by these fears and may be convinced you can never get free.

If you are apprehensive, panic-sticken or feel that the time is not right for you to stop, then let me assure you that your apprehension or panic is caused by fear. That fear is not relieved by cigarettes but created by them. You didn't decide to fall into the nicotine trap. But like all traps, it is designed to ensure that you remain in it. Ask yourself, when you lit those first experimental cigarettes, did you decide to remain a smoker as long as you have? So when are you going to quit? Tomorrow? Next year? Stop kidding yourself! That way you'll remain trapped for life. Why else do you think all these other smokers don't quit before it kills them?

This book was first published by Penguin in 1985 and has been a bestseller every year since then. We now have many years of feedback. As you will soon be reading, the feedback has revealed information that has exceeded my wildest aspirations of the effectiveness of my method. It has also revealed two aspects of EASYWAY that have caused me concern. The second I will be covering later. The first arose from the letters that I have received. I give three typical examples:

'I didn't believe the claims you made and I apologize for doubting you. It was just as easy and enjoyable as you said it would be. I've given copies of your book to all my smoking friends and relatives, but I can't understand why they don't read it.'

'I was given your book eight years ago by an ex-smoking friend. I've just got around to reading it and can't tell you how great it is to be free. My only regret is that I wasted eight years.'

'I've just finished reading EASYWAY. I know it has only been four days, but I feel so great, I know I'll never need to smoke again. I first started to read your book five years ago, got half-way through and panicked. I knew that if I went on reading I would have to stop. Wasn't I silly?'

No, that particular young lady wasn't silly. I've referred to a magic button. Allen Carr's EASYWAY works just like that magic button. Let me make it quite clear, EASYWAY isn't magic, but for me and the millions of ex-smokers who have found it so easy and enjoyable to quit, it seems like magic!

This is the warning. We have a chicken and egg situation. Every smoker wants to quit and every smoker can find it easy and enjoyable to do so. It's only fear that prevents smokers from trying to quit. The greatest gain is to be free from that fear. But you won't be free from it until you complete the book. On the contrary, like the lady in the third example, that fear might increase as you read the book and this might prevent you from finishing it.

You didn't decide to fall into the trap, but be clear in your mind, you won't escape from it unless you make a positive decision to do so. You might already be straining at the leash to quit. On the other hand you might be apprehensive. Either way please bear in mind: YOU HAVE ABSOLUTELY NOTHING TO LOSE!

If at the end of the book you decide that you want to carry on smoking, there is nothing to prevent you from doing so. You don't even have to cut down or stop smoking while you're reading the book, and remember, there's no shock treatment. On the contrary, I have only good news for you. Can you imagine how the Count of Monte Cristo felt when he finally escaped from that prison? That's how I felt when I escaped from the nicotine trap. That's how the millions of ex-smokers who have used my method feel. By the end of the book: THAT'S HOW YOU WILL FEEL! GO FOR IT!

Introduction

'I'M GOING TO CURE THE WORLD OF SMOKING.'

I was talking to my wife. She thought that I had flipped. Understandable if you consider that she had watched me fail on numerous attempts to quit. The most recent had been two years previously. I'd actually survived six months of sheer purgatory before I finally succumbed and lit a cigarette. I'm not ashamed to admit that I cried like a baby. I was crying because I knew that I was condemned to be a smoker for life. I'd put so much effort into that attempt and suffered so much misery that I knew I would never have the strength to go through that ordeal again. I'm not a violent man, but if some patronizing non-smoker had been stupid enough at that moment to suggest to me that all smokers can find it easy to quit, immediately and permanently, I would not have been responsible for my actions. However, I'm convinced that any jury in the world, comprised of smokers only, would have pardoned me on the grounds of justifiable homicide.

Perhaps you too find it impossible to believe that it can be easy for any smoker to quit. If so, I beg you not to cast this book into the rubbish bin. Please trust me. I assure you that even you can find it easy to quit.

Anyway, there I was two years later, having just extinguished what I knew would be my final cigarette, not only telling my wife that I was already a non-smoker, but that I was going to cure the rest of the world. I must admit that at the time I found her scepticism somewhat irritating. However, in no way did it diminish my feeling of exaltation. I suppose that my exhilaration in knowing that I was already a happy non-smoker distorted my perspective somewhat. With the benefit of hindsight, I can sympathize with her attitude. I now understand why Joyce and my close friends and relatives thought I was a candidate for the funny farm.

As I look back on my life, it seems that my whole existence has been a preparation for solving the smoking problem. Even those hateful years of training and practising as a chartered accountant were invaluable in helping me to unravel the mysteries of the smoking trap. They say you can't fool all of the people all of the time, but I believe the tobacco companies have done just that for years. I also believe that I am the first to really understand the smoking trap. If I appear to be arrogant, let me hasten to add that it was no credit to me, just the circumstances of my life.

The momentous day was 15 July 1983. I didn't escape from Colditz, but I imagine those who did felt the same sense of relief and exhilaration as I did when I extinguished that final cigarette. I realized I had discovered something that every smoker was praying for: an easy way to stop smoking.

After testing out the method on smoking friends and relatives, I gave up accountancy and became a full-time consultant, helping other smokers to get free. Another two years later I wrote the first edition of this book. One of my failures, the man I describe in chapter 25, was the inspiration. He visited me twice, and we were both reduced to tears on each occasion. He was so agitated that I couldn't get him to relax enough to absorb what I was saying. I hoped that if I wrote it all down, he could read it in his own good time, as many times as he wanted, and this would help him to absorb the message.

I was in no doubt that EASYWAY would work just as effectively for other smokers as it had done for me. However, when I contemplated putting the method into book form, I was apprehensive. I did my own market research. The comments were not very encouraging:

'How can a book help me to quit? What I need is willpower!'

'How can a book avoid the terrible withdrawal pangs?'

I also had my own doubts. Often at the clinics it became obvious that a client had misunderstood an important point that I was making. I was able to correct the situation. But how would a book be able to do that? I remembered well the times when I studied to qualify as an accountant, when I didn't understand or agree with a particular point in a book, the frustration because you couldn't ask the book to explain. I was also well aware, particularly in these days of television and videos, that many people are not accustomed to reading. Added to all these factors, I had one doubt that overrode all the rest. I wasn't a writer and was very conscious of my limitations in this respect. I was confident that I could sit down face to face with a smoker and convince that smoker how much more enjoyable social occasions will be, how he or she will be better able to concentrate and handle stress as a non-smoker and just how easy and enjoyable the process of quitting can be. But could I transfer that facility to a book? Thankfully the gods were kind to me. I've received tens of thousands of complimentary letters and emails containing comments such as:

'It's the greatest book ever written.'

'You are my guru.'

'You are a genius.'

'You should be knighted.'

'You should be Prime Minister.'

'You are a Saint.'

I hope that I have not allowed such comments to go to my head. I'm fully aware that those comments were made not to compliment me on my literary skills, but in spite of my lack of them. They were made because whether your preference is to read a book or to attend a clinic:

ALLEN CARR'S EASYWAY SYSTEM WORKS!

Not only do we now have a worldwide network of Allen Carr's EASYWAY clinics, but this has been a Penguin best-seller every year since its first publication. It even outsold Harry Potter recently in Norway making it the number one bestseller there of all books, fiction and non-fiction. It has sold over nine million copies in over fifty countries and been translated into over thirty-six different languages.

After approximately a year of running my stop smoking clinics, I thought I had learned everything that it was possible to learn about helping smokers to quit. Amazingly, over twenty years later, I learn something new practically every day. This fact caused me some concern when I was asked to review the first edition after six years of publication. I had a horror that I would have to amend or retract practically everything that I had written.

I needn't have worried. The basic principles of EASY-WAY are as sound today as when I first discovered the method. The beautiful truth is:

IT IS EASY TO STOP

That is a fact. My only difficulty is to convince every smoker of that fact. All of the knowledge that I have accumulated over twenty years is used to enable every smoker to see the light. At the clinics we try to achieve perfection. Every failure hurts us deeply because we know every smoker can find it easy to quit. When smokers fail, they tend to regard it as their failure. We regard it as our failure – we failed to convince those smokers just how easy and enjoyable it is to quit.

I dedicated the first edition to the 16 to 20 per cent of smokers that I had failed to cure. That failure rate was based on the money-back guarantee that we give at our clinics. The average current failure rate of our clinics worldwide is under 10 per cent. That means a success rate of over 90 per cent.

Although I was aware that I had discovered something

marvellous, I never in my wildest dreams expected to achieve such rates. You might well argue that if I genuinely believed that I would cure the world of smoking, I must have expected to achieve 100%.

No, I never ever expected that. Snuff-taking was the previous most popular form of nicotine addiction until it became anti-social and died out. However, there are still a few weirdos who continue to take snuff and, probably, there always will be. Amazingly the Houses of Parliament are one of the last bastions of snuff-taking. I suppose this is not so surprising when you think about it; politicians are generally about a hundred years behind the times! So there will always be a few weirdos who will continue to smoke. I certainly never expected to have to cure every smoker personally.

What I thought would happen was that once I had explained the mysteries of the smoking trap, and dispelled such illusions as:

- Smokers enjoy smoking
- Smokers choose to smoke
- Smoking relieves boredom and stress
- Smoking aids concentration and relaxation
- Smoking is a habit
- It takes willpower to quit
- Once a smoker always a smoker
- Telling smokers that it kills them helps them to quit
- Substitutes, particularly nicotine replacement, help smokers to quit

In particular, when I had dispelled the illusion that it is difficult to quit and that in fact you don't have to go through a transitional period of misery in order to do so, I naively thought that the rest of the world would also see the light and adopt my method.

I thought my chief enemy would be the tobacco industry. Amazingly, my chief obstacles have in fact been the very institutions that I thought would be my greatest allies: the media, the Government, organizations like ASH and QUIT and the established medical profession.

You've probably seen the film *Sister Kenny*. In case you haven't, it is about the time when infantile paralysis or polio was the scourge of our children. I vividly remember that the word engendered the same fear in me as the word cancer does today. The effect of polio was to paralyse the legs and arms and distort the limbs. The established medical treatment was to put those limbs in irons and thus prevent the distortion. The result was paralysis for life.

Sister Kenny believed the irons inhibited recovery and proved a thousand times over that the muscles could be re-educated so that the child could walk again. However, Sister Kenny wasn't a doctor, she was merely a nurse. How dare she dabble in a province that was confined to qualified doctors? It didn't seem to matter that Sister Kenny had found the solution to the problem and had proved her solution to be effective. The children that were treated by Sister Kenny knew she was right, so did their parents, yet the established medical profession not only refused to adopt her methods but actually prevented her from practising. It took Sister Kenny twenty years before the medical profession would accept the obvious.

I first saw that film years before I discovered EASYWAY. The film was very interesting and no doubt there was an element of truth in it. However, it seemed equally obvious that Hollywood had used a large portion of poetic licence.

Sister Kenny couldn't possibly have discovered something that the combined knowledge of medical science had failed to discover. Surely the established medical specialists weren't the dinosaurs they were being portrayed as? How could it possibly have taken them twenty years to accept the facts that were staring them in the face?

They say that fact is stranger than fiction. I apologize for accusing the makers of *Sister Kenny* for using poetic licence. Even in this so-called enlightened age of modern communications, after more than twenty years, even having access to modern communications, I've failed to get my message across. Oh, I've proved my point: the only reason that you are reading this book is because another ex-smoker has recommended it to you. Remember, I don't have the massive financial power of institutions like the BMA, ASH or QUIT. Like Sister Kenny, I'm a lone individual supported only by the wonderful people who have joined my cause and run my clinics around the world. Like her, I'm only famous because my system works. I'm already regarded as the number one guru on helping smokers to quit. Like Sister Kenny I've proved my point. But Sister Kenny proved her point. What good did that serve if the rest of the world was still adopting procedures which were the direct opposite of what they should be?

The last sentences of this book are identical to the original manuscript: 'There is a wind of change in society. A snowball has started that I hope this book will help turn into an avalanche.'

From my remarks above, you might have drawn the conclusion that I am no respecter of the medical profession. Nothing could be further from the truth. One of my sons is a doctor and I know of no finer profession. Indeed we receive more recommendations to our clinics from the medical profession than any other profession, and surprisingly, more of our clients come from the medical profession than any other single profession.

In the early years, I was generally regarded by the medical profession as being somewhere between a charlatan and a quack. In August 1997, I had the great honour to be invited to lecture to the 10th World Conference on Tobacco or Health held in Beijing. I believe that I am the first non-qualified doctor to receive such an honour. The invitation itself was a measure of the progress that I had made. However, I might just as well have been lecturing to a brick wall. Since the nicotine chewing gum and the patch have failed to cure the problem, smokers themselves appear to have realized that you don't get cured from addiction to a drug by prescribing the same drug. It's equivalent to saying to a heroin addict: 'Don't smoke heroin, smoking is dangerous, try injecting it into your veins.' (Don't try this with nicotine, it will kill you instantly.) Because the medical profession, the media and charities like ASH and QUIT haven't a clue about how to help smokers quit, they concentrate on telling smokers what they already know: it's unhealthy, it's filthy and disgusting, it's anti-social and expensive. It never seems to occur to them that smokers do not smoke for the reasons that they shouldn't smoke. The real problem is to remove the reasons that they do.

On national non-smoking days, medical experts always say something like: 'This is the day that every smoker tries to quit!' Every smoker knows that it's the one day in the year that most smokers will smoke twice as much as they usually do and twice as blatantly, because smokers don't like being told what to do, particularly by people who dismiss smokers as mere idiots and don't understand why they smoke.

Because they don't understand smoking or smokers and have no idea how to make it easy to quit, their attitude is: 'Try this method. If it doesn't work try another.' Can you imagine if there were ten different ways of treating appendicitis? Nine of them cure 10 per cent of the patients, which means they kill 90 per cent of them and the tenth way cures 90 per cent. Imagine that knowledge of the tenth method has been available for over twenty years, but the vast majority of the medical profession is still recommending the other nine.

One of the doctors at the Beijing conference raised a very pertinent point that hadn't occurred to me. He pointed out that doctors might well find themselves liable to a legal action for malpractice, by not advising their patients of the best way to quit smoking. Ironically he was a great advocate of Nicotine Replacement Therapy (nicotine gums, patches, etc). I try hard not to be vindictive, but I hope he becomes the first victim of his own suggestion.

Governments regularly waste millions of pounds on shock campaigns trying to persuade youngsters not to get hooked. They might just as well waste it on trying to persuade them that motorbikes can kill you. Do they not realize that youngsters know that one cigarette won't kill them and that no youngster ever expects to get hooked? The link between smoking and lung cancer has been established for over fifty years, yet more youngsters are becoming hooked nowadays than ever before. Youngsters don't need to watch smoking horrors on TV. Smokers tend to avoid such programmes anyway. Practically every youngster in the country has witnessed the actual devastation that smoking causes within their own family. I watched my father and my sister destroyed by the weed; that didn't prevent me from falling into the trap.

I appeared on a national TV programme with a doctor from ASH who had never smoked in her life and had never cured a single smoker, categorically informing the nation how the latest two and a half million pound government shock campaign would prevent youngsters from becoming hooked. If only the government had had the common sense to give that money to me, I could have financed a campaign that would have guaranteed the death of nicotine addiction within a few years.

I truly believe that the snowball has become a football. But after more than twenty years that is still a spit in the ocean. I'm grateful to the millions of ex-smokers who have visited my clinics, read my books, watched my DVDs and have recommended EASYWAY to their friends, relatives and anyone who will listen to them and I pray that you continue to do so. However, the snowball won't become an avalanche until the Government, the medical profession, the media and ASH and QUIT stop recommending methods that make it harder to quit and accept that EASYWAY is not just another method:

BUT THE ONLY SENSIBLE METHOD TO USE

I don't expect you to believe me at this stage, but by the time you have finished the book, you will understand. Even the comparatively few failures that we have say something like:

'I haven't succeeded yet, but your way is better than any I know.'

If when you finish the book, you feel that you owe me a debt of gratitude, you can more than repay that debt. Not just by recommending EASYWAY to your friends, but whenever you see a TV or radio programme, or read a newspaper article advocating some other method, write to them or phone them asking why they aren't advocating Allen Carr's EASYWAY. That will start the avalanche and if I live to witness it, I will die a happy man.

This edition of EASYWAY celebrates the twenty-fifth anniversary of the discovery of the method and gives you the latest technology on just how easy and enjoyable it is to quit smoking. As I sit at my state-of-the-art laptop, it is difficult to believe that the original manuscript of this work was hand written, barely legible, least of all to the writer and then typed up on an ancient Underwood. When I extinguished my final cigarette on 15 July 1983 I knew for certain that I had discovered something that every smoker was searching for: an easy and immediate method to escape from nicotine slavery. What I didn't know for certain was whether I could convince a single smoker, let alone the rest of the world.

With sales in excess of nine million copies, EASYWAY has exceeded my expectations.

It started with just Joyce and I at our home in Raynes Park, London. Today we have a network of over one hundred Allen Carr's EASYWAY clinics in more than thirty-eight countries worldwide.

My thirty years of chain-smoking were a nightmare and I am pleased to have this opportunity to thank my colleagues, my publishers and the millions of ex-smokers who have quit with the help of EASYWAY for making the last twenty-five years seem like paradise.

Do you have a feeling of doom and gloom? Forget it. I've achieved some marvellous things in my life. By far the greatest was to escape from the slavery of nicotine addiction. I escaped twenty-five years ago and still cannot get over the joy of being free. There is no need to feel depressed, nothing bad is happening. On the contrary, you are about to achieve something that every smoker on the planet would love to achieve. TO BE FREE!

Please take a few moments to read the following pages of testimonials.

Allen Carr's EASY WAY To Stop Smoking books and clinics are available in more than 38 countries. Please visit www.allencarr.com for more information or call 0800 389 2115.

UNITED KINGDOM

I can hardly believe that I used to think smoking was cool and glamorous and that life might not be worth living without cigarettes. People tell me I now look years younger. I enjoy social occasions more and handle stress better. I realize now that all my fears about stopping were groundless. In fact I have enjoyed being free from the moment I quit at an Allen Carr's Easyway clinic. *Laura Smith, 31, Berkshire, England, Operations manager*

Allen Carr's Easyway book demolished all the excuses I had for smoking. When I realized that I was simply addicted to nicotine and that the cigarette was simply a nicotine delivery system, I knew I could get free. I thought the withdrawal would be bad but in reality I hardly noticed it and I now feel fantastic to be a non-smoker. *Angela Hollis, 45, Crosby, England, Company secretary*

As a smoker, I thought I had a very stressful work and family life. Because I thought cigarettes relieved stress, I feared I wouldn't be able to cope with life without them. I was amazed that after quitting with Allen Carr's Easyway book, I was noticeably less stressed. I now look back and wonder, 'Where did all that stress go?' As Allen says, it must have been caused by smoking as I'm now far more relaxed as a non-smoker. *Tom Oakes, 31, London, England, Sales director*

At first I couldn't see how a book could possibly help me to quit smoking. But after reading it and deciding when my day of freedom would be it was surprisingly easy. I still can't believe I've done it 18 months on. My life no longer revolves around smoking and I can enjoy life without having to worry 'when will I get my next cigarette.' Absolutely fantastic. *Marian Greenwood, 30, Renfrewshire, Scotland, Accounts administrator*

I was convinced smoking relieved boredom because whenever I was bored, I smoked. It never occurred to me that I was equally bored while smoking until I stopped at one of Allen Carr's Easyway clinics. Now I'm seldom bored because, as a non-smoker, I have far more energy – both physical and mental – to do things which keep me occupied and the most incredible thing is, I never miss cigarettes. *Kathy Davies, 55, Liverpool, England, Grandmother*

I was tortured by the wasted money and the effects on my health through smoking. The 'need' for a cigarette was actually driving me from my warm bed on Saturday mornings when I should have been sleeping. I was 28 but felt tired and lethargic all the time. Thirty cigarettes a day were slowly destroying me. I stopped for a year previously without Allen Carr's Easyway and I eventually caved because I was miserable. The book removed my fears of stopping smoking again and motivated me to try. I feel a hundred times better inside myself and the health benefits were obvious even after only a short time. As described in the book – it was the escape from the slavery that is the best feeling. I am no longer depending on cigarettes to relax me, help me concentrate, relieve boredom or stress. I just see smoking for what it is but I don't want to turn into a self-righteous nag! Now I actually DO feel like a non-smoker. I have gone from being a tetchy and irritated smoker to being calm and relaxed in a matter of weeks. Most people are the opposite when they stop smoking without Allen Carr's Easyway . . . I can't explain it either! *Sarah Cochrane, 29, Co Down, Northern Ireland, Administrative assistant*

I enjoy playing cards. I always used to chain-smoke during games as I was convinced that otherwise I couldn't concentrate and I was terrified that if I quit, I would start losing. I was amazed that after quitting with Allen Carr's Easyway, my concentration improved and I now play better and win more than I ever did as a smoker. *David Brown, 60, London, England, Company director*

I've always been very sociable and gone out a lot to meals, drinks and parties where I smoked like a chimney. I was frightened of stopping because I thought I would never be able to enjoy those situations again. When I quit with Allen Carr's Easyway clinics it was a revelation! I immediately enjoyed them more as a non-smoker and the strange thing is, I've never felt deprived. *Neil Waddington, 28, Huddersfield, England, Recruitment consultant*

As a smoker, I felt like I was being pulled in two opposite directions at the same time. I desperately wanted to stop but I also had an uncontrollable desire to smoke. Previous attempts to quit with willpower with nicotine substitutes were a nightmare and always failed, leaving me even more miserable. Allen Carr's Easyway book was completely different. I had no desire to smoke and stopping was not only easy but I actually enjoyed the process. If I can do it, anybody can! *Angela Murphy, 33, Hampshire, England, Mother and housewife*

I used to block my mind to the bad sides of smoking like the money, saying, 'It's only £5 per packet.' I never confronted the fact that I was spending over £2,000 a year on cigarettes. Since quitting, I've saved an absolute fortune. Amazingly stopping at an Allen Carr's Easyway Clinic was just that: EASY. And I've never had the slightest craving since. *Elaine Williams, 45, Buckinghamshire, England, Head Office manager*

I tried everything to stop smoking but each time I was miserable and irritable and eventually ran out of willpower. I thought the craving would never go. After going to an Allen Carr's Easyway clinic it was completely different right from the start: no craving, no trauma, no tantrum, no misery. In fact the complete opposite: stopping was easy and being free is wonderful. It's definitely one of the best things I've ever done and I'm proud of it! *Elizabeth Pollard, 35, West Sussex, England, Curtain maker*

I tried every substitute I could find including things like nicotine gums, patches, nasal sprays, inhalators, pills, dummy cigarettes, herbal cigarettes, acupuncture and more. None worked. I always felt deprived and miserable and would stuff myself with sweets and chocolate and put on weight. The craving never went. Allen Carr's Easyway was different. I felt no need or desire to substitute as I did not feel I was missing anything and I actually lost weight. I'm now a slimmer and very happy non-smoker. Thanks a million Allen Carr! *Zoe Harmer, 35, Portsmouth, England, Relations assistant*

It was like switching on a light bulb in my brain – all of a sudden everything made sense. Since stopping smoking I have more energy, I'm more patient and even-tempered, my skin looks great, I sleep better – basically I feel fantastic. I thought I was doomed to be a smoker for the rest of my life but now I feel completely re-energized, living and loving life to the full instead of sat indoors watching television every night. I can't put into words what a change Allen Carr made to my life but I will always be immensely grateful to him. *Debra Beazer, 43, Bristol, England, School administrator*

I attended an Allen Carr's Easyway clinic session in Bournemouth. It was incredible considering all you do for five hours is talk about smoking while having cigarette breaks throughout. It was great that we weren't force fed about how awful smoking is for you and all the illnesses and what it does to your body. It is a very effective method and quite unbelievable how it works. You start the session thinking 'it isn't going to work' and by the time you have your last cigarette five hours later you really feel that it is your last one forever. Life is so much easier because I'm not trying to make time for cigarettes while rushing around after the children and all the other bits and pieces that I have to do. My husband attended the clinic as well and he looks so much better for having stopped. I just feel so much better and I don't cough at all anymore. I can spend so much more time with my children as I am not popping out every now and again for a quick ciggie! We are also saving so much money we are putting it into our holiday fund for a trip to the Maldives. It means that we can go on long haul flights without my husband worrying whether he will be able to cope without smoking for such long periods. The world is now our oyster! *Tamsen Minchin, 38, Dorset, England, Housewife*

We don't just receive thousands of unsolicited testimonials from the UK, but from every corner of the globe. For the latest testimonials visit www.allencarr.com and click on 'Read what others say about Allen Carr's Easyway'.

REST OF THE WORLD

ALASKA

While reading the book, I was certain that it wouldn't work, but kept reading, desperate to finally be free. I promised myself I would read the entire book, and do exactly as it suggested. When I quit, I felt a little anxious for about three or four days, and it's been smooth sailing since then. My energy level has soared. I feel so proud that I've finally beat this. The pain I constantly felt in my lungs is starting to diminish. *Jeanette Blalock, 44, Court stenographer*

AUSTRALIA

I used to con myself that smokers were more fun and interesting and that smoking helped me socially. Since I quit with Allen Carr's *EASY WAY To Stop Smoking* DVD, I've realized it was just an excuse. In fact, my social life has improved immensely now that I don't have to rush outside for a smoke and don't stink of tobacco. I now enjoy meals, drinks and parties to the full without feeling stupid or guilty. And the amazing thing is: I NEVER MISS IT! *James French, 37, Financial services executive*

BELARUS

It was amazing – I now go more in for sports, and I have more money! *Tamara Skumpiy, Chief accountant*

BELGIUM

I read the book and attended the Belgian Allen Carr's EASYWAY clinic (paid for by my company) and this made me become a very happy NON-SMOKER. The clinic was fabulous, efficient and successful. No substitutes, no drugs, no problems at all. *Caroline von Hannover, 43, Executive assistant to finance director*

BRAZIL

It's a very good book. It helped me a lot in order to quit smoking. I have much more energy. I've always lifted weights at the gym but the results used to come slowly. Now I can see that the improvements come in a smaller period of time. My strength increased a lot in the past four months. *Josemar Castor, 37, Government employee*

BULGARIA

I was hoping the book would help me because I tried every other method. I believed that the book would help maybe because two of my friends have succeeded stopping thanks to it. I feel happy that I do not smoke anymore. *Elitsa Grancharova, 29, Ecologist, writer, student*

CANADA

I was sceptical about using a book to quit smoking but it worked! I have been smoking since I was seventeen years old and quit a couple of times, one of which lasted three years. I had used nicorette and the patch to quit then. This time around, I had developed a smoker's cough and wasn't feeling as good as I liked. I knew that my symptoms were directly related to smoking. While reading the book, I was still unsure about quitting but I extinguished my last cigarette with the book and haven't lit one since. My smoker's cough is completely gone, I have no more palpitations when I jog. My heart rate is down to less than 60 bpm. Headaches are gone and my self-confidence is back. I feel free! *Brigitte Bouchard, 44, Dental hygienist*

CRETE

Amazing – I never thought I could even think about stopping smoking let alone do it. The book totally changed my way of thinking. All my family have bought me presents as not one of them thought I would ever stop – they think I have been so strong but I've told them I don't deserve the presents, Allen Carr's EASYWAY did it . . . I found it easy – so far I have encouraged four people to buy the book and stop and they also are still non-smokers. I'm healthier, feel so much better about myself, feel cleaner because I don't smell. I can't believe how much time I wasted smoking and worrying about it when it turned out so easy to stop. *Tracey Baines, 41, Administrator*

CYPRUS

I liked the way that Allen approaches the subject from a different angle, really makes you see sense in quitting. I feel so much more alive, relaxed, and happy. I look at other smokers and feel sorry for them. *Nick Cavaye, 36, Salesperson*

ECUADOR

I live in Cuenca and I stopped smoking with Allen Carr's book. It was easy . . . it was amazing. I am free. *Rocio Alcazar*

FRANCE

I was amazed how easy it was to stop smoking with this method. Easy, easy, easy, easy. *Claudine Hoset*

GERMANY

The book worked for me – no pain – no withdrawals. In Germany the book is called *Endlich Nichtraucher*. Everyone knows this book in Germany – everyone knows Allen Carr. *Gerard Schmitzeiger*

GREECE

This book worked for me. It clears up what is happening. It clears up all the lies and the myths about smoking and nicotine. It takes away every fear you have about stopping smoking. I breathe better, I smell better, I am free from the smell. I go out more than before. The fact others smoke (and in Greece everyone does) doesn't have any effect on me. I feel like I have woken up from a nightmare. *Dimitri Tsambrounis, 42, Engineer*

IRAN

YIPPEE! I AM A HAPPY NON-SMOKER! Thank you so much for your beautiful book, I stopped after 35 years by reading the book just once. From the beginning I was full of joy and couldn't wait to finish reading it. I live in Tehran/Iran and the book was sent to me by my daughter who lives in Leeds. Thank you a million times. *Afshin Afshari*

IRELAND

I am most certainly not the type of person that would normally write a testimonial. I am often left wondering about how genuine published testimonials are. Having worked in sales for over ten years I realize their power; they take a potential customer over the bridge to part with their money. I am writing this testimonial for one reason, and one reason only: to let every single reader know that after trying methods beyond belief I finally found the method that worked, a method that came with no post-quit cravings. I drove out of the parking lot of the clinic venue in the confident knowledge that I would sooner eat a bag of coal than light up another cigarette. Try it folks. Just try it. Beyond a shadow of a doubt the best decision I have ever made. *Aidan Parle*

ISRAEL

I was a smoker for thirteen years and now I have stopped . . . thanks to the fabulous book of Allen Carr. The best method the world has found. Thanks Allen, this is a big discovery that will be recorded in history! *Leo Joels*

ITALY

I used the book two years ago — it worked. I have got my breath back, my energy back, and no more smelling like an ashtray. Even sex is better and my self-esteem is boosted!! The method works! *Paolo Coretti*

JAPAN

I REALLY didn't want to smoke again when I finished the book. But when I started the book I didn't think that feeling was possible. I'm amazed still about that . . . *Kenji Nagashima, 36, Teacher*

KAZAKHSTAN

I smoked 20–30 cigarettes per day. I tried to quit before without success . . . five months ago I read Allen's book and it was over with cigarettes. The best was the fact that my wife was so impressed so she has read it too and has finished with cigarettes as well. I would never have believed it if someone had told me that a book could help me quit my addictions but Allen Carr has changed my life and my addictions are now only part of history. *Elchin Abdullayev*

KENYA

It was amazing from the word 'GO'. I felt a real connection with Allen and it was as if he knew exactly what I was feeling, in terms of the smoking, and it made it so much easier to understand the points he was trying to make. I had been smoking for more than ten years and after trying to quit for two years and failing, I had begun to smoke even more. When I got the book I read it in 48 hours and became a 'happy non-smoker by the 48th Hour!' I feel reborn! I have no cravings, I have regained my self-confidence and realize how brainwashed I was to actually think I could not survive without cigarettes. Most of all I am HAPPY, my loved ones are ecstatic and I will be forever grateful to Allen Carr for this book. Now it's my turn to spread the good news in Kenya and Ethiopia and as far as I can go! Thank you! *Sylvia Okwaro, 33, Hotel operations manager*

LATVIA

I was smoking from the age of twelve years old, When I was eighteen I tried to stop without the Allen Carr method. I was sitting at home all the time and eating sweet things but I still ended up smoking again after a few days. My friend advised me to read Allen Carr's book. I read it and I broke away from smoking without any problem! *Elena Matavkina, 21, Student*

LITHUANIA

I became a twenty-a-day smoker, I started to feel quite weak in sports and this gave me my first idea to quit. Several attempts were quite complicated. I quit for a month and afterwards I gained ten extra kilos in weight. Then I started again. I heard about Allen Carr's book from a colleague who had just quit with it and I grabbed it immediately. That evening I became a happy non-smoker. *Evaldas Zvirblis*

MAURITIUS

I started smoking Chesterfield cigarettes when I was twelve years old and by the time I was fifteen I was already a pack-a-day smoker. I had tried various methods of quitting; nicotine patches, gum, cold turkey/ willpower, but never with any success. Each time I tried to stop it was a drama, I felt deprived and miserable without my 'friends' and quickly jumped back on the smoking wagon with great relief and shame. Having started smoking so young I honestly couldn't imagine a life without cigarettes and dreaded having to stop 'one day' and so kept putting it off. I ended up smoking two packs a day. A friend strongly recommended that I buy the book as she and a few of her friends had quit with it. I was very sceptical but decided to give it a try. It was my salvation, I quit the day I finished the book and have never looked back; and I am now a happy non-smoker. I aim to bring the method to Mauritius. *Heidi Houreau*

MEXICO

I want to thank you from the bottom of my heart (and lungs) for saving my life! I have been cigarette-free for almost two years and I will never EVER smoke again. I feel wonderful and thanks to you I have been able to break the curse that had taken over me for fifteen years. A HUGE hug from Mexico. *Luisa Bortoni*

NETHERLANDS

Brilliant – there would have been no other way for me to permanently and definitely stop smoking. It tells you WHY people smoke – something I never really grasped – which is the key to quitting. It had a massive impact on my life – I have more energy – I took on sports again and speed cycling is my favourite hobby. I enjoy my free time now. At work I am much more productive. Like the book claims – quitting only has advantages. I didn't fully realize what a nightmare smoking is till I quit by reading this book. *Thijs Broersma, 33, Manager for oil company*

NEW ZEALAND

It took me two years after receiving Allen Carr's book to pluck up the courage to start reading it. I made all sorts of excuses. It took me ages to read because I was terrified of getting to the end and having to stop. Thankfully I realized that the idea was to smoke while reading it. Incredibly, once I did finish it, my fears had gone and I've been a happy non-smoker ever since. My only regret is that I didn't do it earlier and spare myself those extra years as a smoker. At least I didn't leave it too late and being free from that slavery is such a relief. *Heather Tennant, 46, Data entry assistant*

NORWAY

I found the book very repetitive at first and felt like it was talking to me as if I was stupid, which annoyed me no end. But I realized I had absolutely no argument against Allen's points and soon found that I couldn't put the book down. I stopped smoking easily. The second I finished it – my boyfriend's sister picked it up and read it and stopped smoking too. Now my boyfriend is so jealous of us he is now reading it as well. *Lianne Peters, 32, Farm hand*

PORTUGAL

I read the book – it was easy – end of story. Read it. *Christian Ochoe*

RUMANIA

I read the book – It was like a miracle. I've tried many ways to stop smoking, and with this book I quit so easily – I almost can't believe it. My family is so happy that I quit smoking. *Lupoiu Daniel, 26, Police officer*

RUSSIA

I have never written a letter like this before but to you I have decided to write. I have read the book and now I have not smoked for over four months! It is very important for me! I smoked for fifteen years. Sometimes I tried to stop, but unsuccessfully. I decided that I would have to smoke all my life. Then the book appeared. I did not trust it, I did not think that it was possible to stop smoking after perusal of a book. My female curiosity forced me to read it . . . and the miracle has taken place! I DO NOT SMOKE ANYMORE! I bought some copies for my friends. They too do not smoke now! *Olga Lelka*

SERBIA

I went to Allen Carr's EASYWAY To Stop Smoking and after five hours – I stopped smoking. No-one is more amazed than I am! *Martija Snerchich*

SLOVAKIA

The book describes how smoking addiction works. When I understood it – it was easy to stop smoking. I feel much more free, I have much more confidence in myself and I am very proud to be a non-smoker after eighteen years of smoking forty cigarettes a day. *N Gasaj, 36, Historian*

SOUTH AFRICA

I bought myself Allen Carr's *EASY WAY To Stop Smoking* and I am now a happy non-smoker. It took me some time to finish the book, but in the end I did it and I haven't looked back – I even 'endured' the stress of having an accident without starting smoking again. I found that since I stopped smoking I have so much more energy, I have lost weight and started cycling and playing netball again. *Lizelle Brighton*

SPAIN

I think the book was very helpful to make me understand why I started smoking and that I was strong enough to leave it behind. I just thought I had nothing to lose trying this method and I did it successfully. I feel very good, I feel I can do more things than I thought I could. I am able to do more exercise and breathe better. My life has changed in a better way because I feel free now. *Sonia Vila Sanchez, 31, Nurse*

SWEDEN

I loved the book because it certainly feels like a human had written it. Someone who is eager to share his new-found wisdom (or whatever you want to call it). It is not a cold, non-emotional doctor who just drops fact after fact. That's what I appreciated the most – the warmth and commitment. I enjoy the freedom to be able to think on other things – smoking took so much of my time. Also I cough less and have better sleep. And the big difference from the other times I tried to quit – I do not feel deprived – I feel FREE! *Natte Hillerberg, 19, Student*

SWITZERLAND

A friend of mine had read the book – but I was lazy and so went to the Allen Carr's EASYWAY To Stop Smoking clinic instead. I remember sitting thinking, 'This is not going to work on me,' but it did. My life is changed forever. Best of all – it was easy and I do not feel like I am missing out on anything by not smoking. *Leo Bauhmann*

THAILAND

After twenty-five years I thought it impossible to give up and certainly thought that there was no 'easy way'. However, at some point whilst reading the book something clicked and I consciously remember extinguishing my last cigarette. The strange thing is I feel somewhat stunned, because it's so effective – if that makes sense. Many people I know are equally as stunned and have trouble coming to terms with the fact that I simply stopped. Some of them are using NRT and are now addicted to nicotine gum. They refuse to admit that, of course. To be honest, I find the whole thing somewhat eerie – because it was so easy! *Michael White, 43, Manager*

TUNISIA

I do not understand how it works – I was very sceptical that a book could stop me from smoking. No way! Here I am now – a non-smoker – and it was easy. I do not believe in magic or miracles – but that is what it feels like. *Asaf Muthi*

TURKEY

The book was powerful and completely changed my perceptions of my need to smoke by turning them on their head. The image most meaningful to me was that smoking a cigarette takes you back to the level of comfort that non-smokers are at all the time. I feel much less stressed. I was always stressed when I was going somewhere where I knew I couldn't smoke and would chain-smoke before leaving for a flight, or for a bus, or for someone's house. It was then embarrassing to arrive and know that I smelt of cigarettes. I felt bad picking up my friends' babies if I had been smoking, due to the smell and the toxic fumes still on my breath. I really feel free now and look with pity at all those smokers stood outside at the airport, the train stations, the bus stations, the restaurants and bars. I started smoking aged fifteen and am now thirty-four. I am so glad I have stopped and am no longer terrified that every sore throat I get is throat cancer, every cough is something more serious. My asthma which started when I was eighteen has now completely gone. I feel great relief, much less stress and no longer ashamed of my house and me smelling awful. *V Sayar, 34, Marketing executive*

UKRAINE

I've just become the happiest person in the world! I STOPPED SMOK-ING. Years of addiction finally finished. I've just read the book by Allen Carr. I've become ABSOLUTELY FREE. I'm a political scientist and psychologist, so I felt a lot of scepticism when starting to read this book. But now I'm free. *Maria Sergeivena*

USA

I am amazed at how easy it was. After many years of smoking and trying to quit using the patch, lozenge, inhaler, hypnotism, etc, I read the book and quit right away and it was very easy to do. It's an excellent method that should be shared world-wide with all people wanting to quit. I immediately started to feel better. I have more energy and I'm walking every day now. My kids are happy that I'm not outside smoking all the time and I have more time to get things done in my life now that I'm not a prisoner. I stopped wheezing and coughing within the first week and my skin looks better. It has changed my life and I know I will never go back to it again. *Joanne Pele, 42, VP of operations*

If you have any questions while you read this book, you are very welcome to contact your nearest Allen Carr's EASYWAY To Stop Smoking Clinic – free of charge – for clarification, guidance, or advice.

0800 389 2115 or visit www.allencarr.com

1 The Worst Nicotine Addict I Have Yet to Meet

Perhaps I should begin by describing my competence for writing this book. No, I am not a doctor or a psychiatrist; my qualifications are far more appropriate. I spent thirty-three years of my life as a confirmed smoker. In the later years I smoked a hundred a day on a bad day, and never less than sixty.

I made dozens of attempts to stop. I once stopped for six months, and I was still climbing the wall, still standing near smokers trying to get a whiff of the tobacco.

With most smokers, on the health side, it's a question of 'I'll stop before it happens to me.' I had reached the stage where I knew it was killing me. I had a permanent headache with the pressure of the constant coughing. I could feel the continuous throbbing in the vein that runs vertically down the centre of my forehead, and I honestly believed that any moment there would be an explosion in my head and I would die from a brain haemorrhage. It bothered me, but it still didn't stop me.

I had reached the stage where I gave up even trying to stop. It was not so much that I enjoyed smoking. At some time in their lives most smokers have suffered from the illusion that they enjoy the odd cigarette; but I never suffered from that illusion. I have always detested the taste and smell, but I thought a cigarette helped me to relax. It gave me courage and confidence, and I was always miserable when I tried to stop, never being able to visualize an enjoyable life without a cigarette.

Eventually my wife sent me to a hypnotherapist. I must confess that I was completely sceptical, knowing nothing about hypnosis in those days and having visions of a Svengali-type figure with piercing eyes and a waving pendulum. I suffered many of the usual illusions that smokers have about smoking except one – I knew that I wasn't a weak-willed person. I was in control of all other aspects of my life but cigarettes controlled me. I thought that hypnosis involved the forcing of wills, and although I was not obstructive (like most smokers, I dearly wanted to stop), I thought no one was going to kid me that I didn't need a smoke.

The whole session appeared to be a waste of time. The hypnotherapist tried to make me lift my arms and do various other things. Nothing appeared to be working properly. I didn't lose consciousness. I didn't go into a trance, or at least I didn't think I did, and yet after that session not only did I stop smoking but I actually enjoyed the process even during the withdrawal period.

Now, before you go rushing off to see a hypnotherapist, let me make something quite clear. Hypnotherapy is a means of communication. If the wrong message is communicated, you won't stop smoking. I'm loath to criticize the man whom I consulted because I would be dead by now if I hadn't seen him. But it was in spite of him, not because of him. Neither do I wish to appear to be knocking hypnotherapy; on the contrary, we use it as part of our programme at our clinics. It is the power of suggestion and a powerful force that can be used for good or evil. Don't ever consult a hypnotherapist unless he or she has been personally recommended by someone you respect and trust.

During those awful years as a smoker I thought that my life depended on cigarettes, and I was prepared to die rather than be without them. Today people ask me whether I ever have the odd pang. The answer is, 'Never, never, never' – just the reverse. I've had a marvellous life. If I had died through smoking, I couldn't have complained. I have been a very lucky man, but the most marvellous thing that has ever happened to me is being freed from that nightmare, that slavery of having to go through life systematically destroying my own body and paying through the nose for the privilege.

Let me make it quite clear from the beginning: I am not a mystical figure. I do not believe in magicians or fairies. I have a scientific brain, and I couldn't understand what appeared to me like magic. I started reading up on hypnosis and on smoking. Nothing I read seemed to explain the miracle that had happened. Why had it been so ridiculously easy to stop, whereas previously it had been weeks of black depression?

It took me a long time to work it all out, basically because I was going about it back to front. I was trying to work out why it had been so *easy* to stop, whereas the real problem is trying to explain why smokers usually find it so *difficult*. Smokers talk about the terrible withdrawal pangs, but when I looked back and tried to remember those awful pangs, they didn't exist for me. There was no physical pain. It was all in the mind.

My full-time profession is now helping other smokers to get free. I'm very, very successful and my clinics and books have helped to cure millions of smokers. Let me emphasize from the start: there is no such thing as a confirmed smoker.

I have still not met anybody who was as badly hooked (or, rather, *thought* he was as badly hooked) as myself. Anybody can not only stop smoking but also find it easy. It is basically fear that keeps us smoking: the fear that life will never be quite as enjoyable without cigarettes and the fear of feeling deprived. In fact, nothing could be further from the truth. Not only is life just as enjoyable without them but it is infinitely more so in so many ways and extra health, energy and wealth are the least of the advantages.

All smokers can find it easy to stop – even you! All you have to do is read the rest of the book with an open mind. The more you can understand, the easier you will find it. Even if you do not understand every word, provided you follow the instructions you will find it easy. Most important of all, you will not go through life moping for cigarettes or feeling deprived. The only mystery will be why you did it for so long.

Let me issue a warning. There are only two reasons for failure with my method:

1. **Failure to Carry Out Instructions.** Some people find it annoying that I am so dogmatic about certain recommendations. For example, I will tell you not to try cutting down or using substitutes like sweets, chewing gum, etc. I will also explain why so-called Nicotine Replacement Therapy (nicotine gums, patches, nasal sprays, inhalators, pills, etc) simply keeps you hooked. The reason why I am so dogmatic is because I know my subject. I do not deny that there are many people who have succeeded in stopping after using such ruses, but they have succeeded in spite of, not because of them. There are people who can make love standing on a hammock, but it is not the easiest way.

Everything I tell you has a purpose: to make it easy to stop and thereby ensure success.

2. **Failure to Understand.** Do not take anything for granted. Question not only what I tell you but also your own views and what society has taught you about smoking. For example, those of you who think it is just a habit, ask yourselves why other habits, some of them enjoyable ones, are easy to break, yet a habit that tastes awful, costs us a fortune and kills us is so difficult to break. Those of you who think you enjoy a cigarette, ask yourselves why other things in life, which are infinitely more enjoyable, you can take or leave. Why do you *have* to have the cigarette and panic sets in if you don't?

2 The Easy Method

The object of this book is to get you into the frame of mind in which, instead of the normal method of stopping whereby you start off with the feeling that you are climbing Mount Everest and spend the next few weeks craving a cigarette and envying other smokers, you start right away with a feeling of elation, as if you had been cured of a terrible disease. From then on, the further you go through life the more you will look at cigarettes and wonder how you ever smoked them in the first place. You will look at smokers with pity as opposed to envy.

Provided that you are not a non-smoker or an ex-smoker, it is essential to keep smoking until you have finished the book completely. This may appear to be a contradiction. Later I shall be explaining that cigarettes do absolutely nothing for you at all. In fact, one of the many conundrums about smoking is that when we are actually smoking a cigarette, we look at it and wonder why we are doing it. It is only when we have been deprived that the cigarette becomes precious. However, let us accept that, whether you like it or not, you believe you are hooked. When you believe you are hooked, you can never be completely relaxed or concentrate properly unless you are smoking. So do not attempt to stop smoking before you have finished the whole book. As you read further your desire to smoke will gradually be reduced. Do not go off half-cocked; this could be fatal. Remember, all you have to do is to follow the instructions.

With the benefit of more than twenty years' feedback since the book's original publication, apart from chapter 28, 'Timing', this instruction to continue to smoke until you have completed the book has caused me more frustration than any other. When I first stopped smoking, many of my relatives and friends stopped, purely because I had done it. They thought, 'If he can do it, anybody can.' Over the years, by dropping little hints I managed to persuade the ones that hadn't stopped to realize just how nice it is to be free! When the book was first printed I gave copies to the hard core who were still puffing away. I worked on the basis that, even if it were the most boring book ever written, they would still read it, if only because it had been written by a friend. I was surprised and hurt to learn that, months later, they hadn't bothered to finish the book. I even discovered that the original copy I had signed and given to someone who was then my closest friend had not only been ignored but actually given away. I was hurt at the time, but I had overlooked the dreadful fear that slavery to the weed instills in the smoker. It can transcend friendship. I nearly provoked a divorce because of it. My mother once said to my wife, 'Why don't you threaten to leave him if he doesn't stop smoking?' My wife said, 'Because he'd leave me if I did.' I'm ashamed to admit it, but I believe she was right, such is the fear that smoking creates. I now realize that many smokers don't finish the book because they feel they have got to stop smoking when they do. Some deliberately read only one line a day in order to postpone the evil day. Now I am fully aware that many readers are having their arms twisted, by people that love them, to read the book. Look at it this way: what have you got to lose? If you don't stop at the end of the book, you are no worse off than you are now. YOU HAVE ABSOLUTELY NOTHING TO LOSE AND SO MUCH TO GAIN! Incidentally, if you have not smoked for a few days or weeks but are not sure whether you are a smoker, an ex-smoker or a non-smoker, then don't smoke while you read. In fact, you are already a non-smoker. All we've now got to do is to let your brain catch up with your body. By the end of the book you'll be a happy non-smoker.

Basically my method is the complete opposite of the normal method of trying to stop. The *normal* method is to list the considerable disadvantages of smoking and say, 'If only I can go long enough without a cigarette, eventually the desire to smoke will go. I can then enjoy life again, free of slavery to the weed.'

This is the logical way to go about it, and thousands of smokers are stopping every day using variations of this method. However, it is very difficult to succeed using this method for the following reasons:

1. Stopping smoking is not the real problem. Every time you put a cigarette out you stop smoking. You may have powerful reasons on day one to say, 'I do not want to smoke any more' – all smokers have, every day of their lives, and the reasons are more powerful than you can possibly imagine. The real problem is day two, day ten or day ten thousand, when in a weak moment, an inebriated moment or even a strong moment you have one cigarette, and because it is partly drug addiction you then want another, and suddenly you are a smoker again.

2. The health scares should stop us. Our rational minds say, 'Stop doing it. You are a fool,' but in fact they make it harder. We smoke, for example, when we are nervous. Tell smokers that it is killing them, and the first thing they will do is to light a cigarette. There are more dog ends outside the Royal Marsden Hospital, the United Kingdom's foremost cancer treatment establishment, than any other hospital in the country.

3. All reasons for stopping actually make it harder for two other reasons. *First*, they create a sense of sacrifice. We are always being forced to give up our little friend or prop or vice or pleasure, whichever way the smoker sees it. *Secondly*, they create a 'blind'. We do not smoke for the reasons we should stop. The real question is 'Why do we want or need to do it?'

The Easy Method is basically this: initially to forget the reasons we'd like to stop, to face the cigarette problem and to ask ourselves the following questions:

1. What is it doing for me?
2. Do I actually enjoy it?
3. Do I really need to go through life paying through the nose just to stick these things in my mouth and suffocate myself?

The beautiful truth is that it does absolutely nothing for you at all. Let me make it quite clear, I do not mean that the disadvantages of being a smoker outweigh the advantages; all smokers know that all their lives. I mean there are not *any* advantages from smoking. The only advantage it ever had was the social 'plus'; nowadays even smokers themselves regard it as antisocial.

Most smokers find it necessary to rationalize why they smoke, but the reasons are all fallacies and illusions. The first thing we are going to do is to remove these fallacies and illusions. In fact, you will realize that there is nothing to give up. Not only is there nothing to give up but there are marvellous, positive gains from being a non-smoker, and health and money are only two of these gains. Once the illusion that life will never be quite as enjoyable without the cigarette is removed, once you realize that not only is life just as enjoyable without it but infinitely more so, once the feeling of being deprived or of missing out is eradicated, then we can go back to reconsider the health and money – and the dozens of other reasons for stopping smoking. These realizations will become positive additional aids to help you achieve what you really desire – to enjoy the whole of your life free from the slavery of the weed.

3 Why is it Difficult to Stop?

As I explained earlier, I got interested in this subject because of my own addiction. When I finally stopped it was like magic. When I had previously tried to stop there were weeks of black depression. There would be odd days when I was comparatively cheerful but the next day back with the depression. It was like clawing your way out of a slippery pit, you feel you are near the top, you see the sunshine and then find yourself sliding down again. Eventually you light that cigarette, it tastes awful and you try to work out why you have to do it.

One of the questions we always ask smokers prior to our clinic sessions is 'Do you want to stop smoking?' In a way it is a stupid question. All smokers would love to stop smoking. If you say to the most confirmed smoker, 'If you could go back to the time before you became hooked, with the knowledge you have now, would you have started smoking?', 'NO WAY' is the reply.

Say to the most confirmed smoker – someone who doesn't think that it injures his health, who is not worried about the social stigma and who can afford it (there are not many about these days) – 'Do you encourage your children to smoke?', 'NO WAY' is the reply.

All smokers feel that something evil has got possession of

them. In the early days it is a question of 'I am going to stop, not today but tomorrow.' Eventually we get to the stage where we think either that we haven't got the willpower or that there is something inherent in the cigarette that we must have in order to enjoy life.

As I said previously, the problem is not explaining why it is easy to stop; *it is explaining why it is difficult*. In fact, the real problem is explaining why anybody does it in the first place or why, at one time, over 60 per cent of the population were smoking.

The whole business of smoking is an extraordinary enigma. The only reason we get on to it is because of the thousands of people already doing it. Yet every one of them wishes he or she had not started in the first place, telling us that it is a waste of time and money. We cannot quite believe they are not enjoying it. We associate it with being grown up and work hard to become hooked ourselves. We then spend the rest of our lives telling our own children not to do it and trying to quit ourselves.

We also spend the rest of our lives paying through the nose. The average twenty-a-day smoker in the UK spends at least £75,000 in his or her lifetime on cigarettes. What do we do with that money? (It wouldn't be so bad if we threw it down the drain.) We actually use it systematically to congest our lungs with cancerous tars, progressively to clutter up and poison our blood vessels. Each day we are increasingly starving every muscle and organ of our bodies of oxygen, so that each day we become more lethargic. We sentence ourselves to a lifetime of filth, bad breath, stained teeth, burnt clothes, filthy ashtrays and the foul smell of stale tobacco. It is a lifetime of slavery. We spend most of our lives in situations in which we are forbidden to smoke (work, restaurants, shops, bars, churches, hospitals, schools, trains, theatres, etc) or, when we are trying to cut down and stop, feeling deprived. The rest of our smoking lives is spent in situations where we are allowed to smoke but wish we didn't have to. What sort of hobby is it that when you are doing it you wish you weren't, and when you are not doing it you crave it? It's a lifetime of being treated by half of society like some sort of leper and, worst of all, a lifetime of an otherwise intelligent, rational human being going through life in contempt. The smoker despises himself, every Budget Day, every National No-Smoking Day, every time he inadvertently reads the government health warning or there is a cancer scare or a bad-breath campaign, every time he gets congested or has a pain in the chest, every time he is the lone smoker in company with non-smokers. Having to go through life with these awful black shadows at the back of his mind, what does he get out of it? ABSOLUTELY NOTHING! Pleasure? Enjoyment? Relaxation? A prop? A boost? All illusions, unless you consider the wearing of tight shoes to enjoy the removal of them as some sort of pleasure!

As I have said, the real problem is trying to explain not only why smokers find it difficult to stop but why anybody does it at all.

You are probably saying, 'That's all very well. I know this, but once you are hooked on these things it is very difficult to stop.' But why is it so difficult, and why do we have to do it? Smokers search for the answer to these questions all of their lives.

Some say it is because of the powerful withdrawal symptoms. In fact, the actual withdrawal symptoms from nicotine are so mild (see chapter 6) that most smokers have lived and died without ever realizing they are drug addicts.

Some say cigarettes are very enjoyable. They aren't. They are filthy, disgusting objects. Ask any smoker who thinks he smokes only because he enjoys a cigarette if, when he hasn't got his own brand and can only obtain a brand he finds distasteful, he stops smoking? Smokers would rather smoke old rope than not smoke at all. Enjoyment has nothing to do with it. I enjoy lobster but I never got to the stage where I had to have twenty lobsters hanging around my neck. With other things in life we enjoy them whilst we are doing them but we don't sit around feeling deprived when we are not.

Some search for deep psychological reasons, the 'Freudian syndrome', 'the child at the mother's breast'. Really it is just the reverse. The usual reason why we start smoking is to show we are grown up and mature. If we had to suck a dummy in public, we would die of embarrassment.

Some think it is the reverse, the macho effect of breathing smoke or fire down your nostrils. Again this argument has no substance. A burning cigarette in the ear would appear ridiculous. How much more ridiculous to breathe cancer-triggering tars into your lungs.

Some say, 'It is something to do with my hands!' So, why light it?

'It is oral satisfaction.' So, why light it?

'It is the feeling of the smoke going into my lungs.' An awful feeling – it is called suffocation.

Many believe smoking relieves boredom. This is also a fallacy. Boredom is a frame of mind. There is nothing inter-esting about a cigarette.

For thirty-three years my reason was that it relaxed me, gave me confidence and courage. I also knew it was killing me and costing me a fortune. Why didn't I go to my doctor and ask him for an alternative to relax me and give me courage and confidence? I didn't go because I knew he would suggest an alternative. It wasn't my reason; it was my excuse.

Some say they only do it because their friends do it. Are you really that stupid? If so, just pray that your friends don't start cutting their heads off to cure a headache!

Most smokers who think about it eventually come to the conclusion that it is just a habit. This is not really an explanation but, having discounted all the usual rational explanations, it appears to be the only remaining excuse. Unfortunately, this explanation is equally illogical. Every day of our lives we change habits, and some of them are very enjoyable. We have been brainwashed to believe that smoking is a habit and that habits are difficult to break. Are habits difficult to break? In the UK we are in the habit of driving on the left side of the road. Yet when we drive on the Continent or in the United States, we immediately break that habit with hardly any aggravation whatsoever. It is clearly a fallacy that habits are hard to break.

So why do we find it difficult to break a habit that tastes awful, that kills us, that costs us a fortune, that is filthy and disgusting and that we would love to break anyway, when all we have to do is to stop doing it? The answer is that smoking is not habit: IT IS NICOTINE ADDICTION! That is why it appears to be so difficult to 'give up'. Perhaps you feel this explanation explains why it *is* difficult to 'give up'? It does explain why most smokers find it difficult to 'give up'. That is because they do not understand drug addiction. The main reason is that smokers are convinced that they get some genuine pleasure and/or crutch from smoking and believe that they are making a genuine sacrifice if they quit.

The beautiful truth is that once you understand nicotine

addiction and the true reasons why you smoke, you will stop doing it – just like that – and within three weeks the only mystery will be why you found it necessary to smoke as long as you have, and why you cannot persuade other smokers HOW NICE IT IS TO BE A NON-SMOKER!

4 The Sinister Trap

Smoking is the most subtle, sinister trap that man and nature have combined to devise. What gets us into it in the first place? The thousands of adults who are already doing it. They even warn us that it's a filthy, disgusting habit that will eventually destroy us and cost us a fortune, but we cannot believe that they are not enjoying it. One of the many pathetic aspects of smoking is how hard we have to work in order to become hooked.

It is the only trap in nature which has no lure, no piece of cheese. The thing that springs the trap is not that cigarettes taste so marvellous; it's that they taste so awful. If that first cigarette tasted marvellous, alarms bells would ring and, as intelligent human beings, we could then understand why half the adult population was systematically paying through the nose to poison itself. But because that first cigarette tastes awful, our young minds are reassured that we will never become hooked, and we think that because we are not enjoying them we can stop whenever we want to.

It is the only drug in nature that prevents you from achieving your aim. Boys usually start because they want to appear tough – it is the Humphrey Bogart/Clint Eastwood/Bruce Willis image. The last thing you feel with the first cigarette is tough.

You dare not inhale, and if you have too many, you start to feel dizzy, then sick. All you want to do is get away from the other boys and throw the filthy things away.

With women, the aim is to be the sophisticated modern young lady. We have all seen them taking little puffs on a cigarette, looking absolutely ridiculous. By the time the boys have learnt to look tough and the girls have learnt to look sophisticated, they wish they had never started in the first place. I wonder whether women ever look sophisticated when they smoke, or whether this is a figment of our imaginations created by cigarette adverts. It seems to me that there is no intermediary stage between the obvious learner and 'Fag-ash Lil'.

We then spend the rest of our lives trying to explain to ourselves why we do it, telling our children not to get caught and, at odd times, trying to escape ourselves.

The trap is so designed that we try to stop only when we have stress in our lives, whether it be health, shortage of money or just plain being made to feel like a leper.

As soon as we stop, we have more stress (the fearful withdrawal pangs of nicotine) and the thing that we rely on to relieve stress (our old prop, the cigarette) we now must do without.

After a few days of torture we decide that we have picked the wrong time. We must wait for a period without stress, and as soon as that arrives the reason for stopping vanishes. Of course, that period will never arrive because, in the first place, we think that our lives tend to become more and more stressful. As we leave the protection of our parents, the natural process is setting up home, mortgages, babies, more responsible jobs, etc, etc. This is also an illusion. The truth is that the most stressful periods for any creature are early childhood and adolescence. We tend to confuse responsibility with stress. Smokers' lives automatically become more stressful because tobacco does not relax you or relieve stress, as society tries to make you believe. Just the reverse: it actually causes you to become more nervous and stressed.

Even those smokers who do quit (most do, one or more times during their lives) can go on to lead perfectly happy lives yet suddenly become hooked again.

The whole business of smoking is like wandering into a giant maze. As soon as we enter the maze our minds become misted and clouded, and we spend the rest of our lives trying to escape. Many of us eventually do, only to find that we get trapped again at a later date.

I spent thirty-three years trying to escape from that maze. Like all smokers, I couldn't understand it. However, due to a combination of unusual circumstances, none of which reflects any credit on me, I wanted to know why previously it had been so desperately difficult to stop and yet, when I finally did, it was not only easy but enjoyable.

Since stopping smoking my hobby and, later, my profession has been to resolve the many conundrums associated with smoking. It is a complex and fascinating puzzle and, like the Rubik Cube, can appear practically impossible to solve. However, like all complicated puzzles, if you know the solution, it is easy! I have the solution to stopping smoking easily. I will lead you out of the maze and ensure that you never wander into it again. All you have to do is *follow the instructions*. If you take a wrong turn, the rest of the instructions will be pointless.

Let me emphasize that anybody can find it easy to stop smoking, but first we need to establish the facts. No, I do not mean the scare facts. I know you are already aware of them.

There is already enough information on the evils of smoking. If that was going to stop you, you would already have stopped. I mean, why do we find it difficult to stop? In order to answer this question we need to know the real reason why we are still smoking.

5 Why Do We Carry on Smoking?

We all start smoking for stupid reasons, usually social pressures or social occasions, but, once we feel we are becoming hooked, why do we carry on smoking?

No regular smoker knows why he or she smokes. If smokers knew the true reason, they would stop doing it. I have asked the question of thousands of smokers during my consultations. The true answer is the same for all smokers, but the variety of replies is infinite. I find this part of the consultation the most amusing and at the same time the most pathetic.

All smokers know in their heart of hearts that they are mugs. They know that they had no need to smoke before they became hooked. Most of them can remember that their first cigarette tasted awful and that they had to work hard in order to become hooked. The most annoying part is that they sense that non-smokers are not missing anything and that they are laughing at them (it is difficult not to on Budget Day).

However, smokers are intelligent, rational human beings. They know that they are taking enormous health risks and that they spend a fortune on cigarettes in their lifetime. Therefore it is necessary for them to have a rational explanation to justify themselves.

The actual reason why smokers continue to smoke is a subtle combination of the factors that I will elaborate in the next two chapters. They are:

1. NICOTINE ADDICTION
2. BRAINWASHING

6
Nicotine Addiction

Nicotine, a colourless, oily compound, is the drug contained in tobacco that addicts the smoker. It is the fastest addictive drug known to mankind, and it can take just one cigarette to become hooked.

Every puff on a cigarette delivers, via the lungs to the brain, a small dose of nicotine that acts more rapidly than the dose of heroin the addict injects into his veins.

If there are twenty puffs for you in a cigarette, you receive twenty doses of the drug with just one cigarette.

Nicotine is a quick-acting drug, and levels in the bloodstream fall quickly to about half within thirty minutes of smoking a cigarette and to a quarter within an hour of finishing a cigarette. This explains why most smokers average about twenty per day.

As soon as the smoker extinguishes the cigarette, the nicotine rapidly starts to leave the body and the smoker begins to suffer withdrawal pangs.

I must at this point dispel a common illusion that smokers have about withdrawal pangs. Smokers think that withdrawal pangs are the terrible trauma they suffer when they try or are forced to stop smoking. These are, in fact, mainly mental;

the smoker is feeling deprived of his pleasure or prop. I will explain more about this later.

The actual pangs of withdrawal from nicotine are so subtle that most smokers have lived and died without even realizing they are drug addicts. When we use the term 'nicotine addict' we think we just 'got into the habit'. Most smokers have a horror of drugs, yet that's exactly what they are – drug addicts. Fortunately it is an easy drug to kick, but you need first to accept that you are addicted. This point was quite a revelation when this book was first published. Now it is universally accepted.

There is no physical pain in the withdrawal from nicotine. It is merely an empty, restless feeling, the feeling that something is missing, which is why many smokers think it is something to do with their hands. If it is prolonged, the smoker becomes nervous, insecure, agitated, lacking in confidence and irritable. It is like hunger – for a poison, NICOTINE.

Within seven seconds of lighting a cigarette fresh nicotine is supplied and the craving ends, resulting in the feeling of relaxation and confidence that the cigarette appears to give to the smoker.

In the early days, when we first start smoking, the withdrawal pangs and their relief are so slight that we are not even aware that they exist. When we begin to smoke regularly we think it is because we've either come to enjoy it or got into the 'habit'. The truth is we're already hooked; we do not realize it, but that little nicotine monster is already inside us and every now and again we have to feed it.

All smokers start smoking for stupid reasons. Nobody has to. The only reason why anybody continues smoking, whether they be a casual or heavy smoker, is to feed that little monster.

The whole business of smoking is a series of conundrums. All smokers know at heart that they are mugs and have been trapped by something evil. However, I think the most pathetic aspect about smoking is that the enjoyment that the smoker gets from a cigarette is the pleasure of trying to get back to the state of peace, tranquility and confidence that his body had before he became hooked in the first place.

You know that feeling when a neighbour's burglar alarm has been ringing all day, or there has been some other minor, persistent aggravation. Then the noise suddenly stops – that marvellous feeling of peace and tranquillity is experienced. It is not really peace but the ending of the aggravation.

Before we start the nicotine chain, our bodies are complete. We then force nicotine into the body, and when we put that cigarette out and the nicotine starts to leave, we suffer withdrawal pangs – not physical pain, just an empty feeling. We are not even aware that it exists, but it is like a dripping tap inside our bodies. Our rational minds do not understand it. They do not need to. All we know is that we want a cigarette, and when we light it the craving goes, and for the moment we are content and confident again just as we were before we became addicted. However, the satisfaction is only temporary because, in order to relieve the craving, you have to put more nicotine into the body. As soon as you extinguish that cigarette the craving starts again, and so the chain goes on. It is a chain for life – UNLESS YOU BREAK IT.

The whole business of smoking is like wearing tight shoes just to obtain the pleasure you feel when you take them off.

There are three main reasons why smokers cannot see things that way.

1. From birth we have been subjected to massive brainwashing telling us that smokers receive immense pleasure and/or a crutch from smoking. Why should we not believe it? Why else would smokers waste all that money and take such horrendous risks?
2. Because the physical withdrawal from nicotine involves no actual pain but is merely an empty, insecure feeling, inseparable from hunger or normal stress, and because those are the very times that we tend to light up, we tend to regard the feeling as normal.
3. However the main reason that smokers fail to see smoking in its true light is because it works back to front. It's when you are not smoking that you suffer that empty feeling, but because the process of getting hooked is very subtle and gradual in the early days, we regard that feeling as normal and don't blame it on the previous cigarette. The moment you light up, you get an almost immediate boost or buzz and do actually feel less nervous or more relaxed, and the cigarette gets the credit.

It is this reverse process that makes all drugs difficult to kick. Picture the panic state of a heroin addict who has no heroin. Now picture the utter joy when that addict can finally plunge a hypodermic needle into his vein. Can you visualize someone actually getting pleasure by injecting themselves, or does the mere thought fill you with horror? Non-heroin addicts don't suffer that panic feeling. The heroin doesn't relieve it. On the contrary, it causes it. Non-smokers don't suffer the empty feeling of needing a cigarette or start to panic when the supply runs out. Non-smokers cannot understand how smokers can possibly obtain pleasure from sticking those filthy things in their mouths, setting light to them and actually inhaling the filth into their lungs. And do you know something? Smokers cannot understand why they do it either.

We talk about smoking being relaxing or giving satisfaction. But how can you be satisfied unless you were dissatisfied in the first place? Why don't non-smokers suffer from this dissatisfied state and why, after a meal, when non-smokers are completely relaxed, are smokers completely unrelaxed until they have satisfied that little nicotine monster?

Forgive me if I dwell on this subject for a moment. The main reason that smokers find it difficult to quit is that they believe that they are giving up a genuine pleasure or crutch. It is absolutely essential to understand that you are giving up nothing whatsoever.

The best way to understand the subtleties of the nicotine trap is to compare it with eating. If we are in the habit of eating regular meals, we are not aware of being hungry between meals. Only if the meal is delayed are we aware of being hungry, and even then, there is no physical pain, just an empty, insecure feeling which we know as: 'I need to eat.' And the process of satisfying our hunger is a very pleasant pastime.

Smoking appears to be almost identical. The empty, insecure feeling which we know as: 'wanting or needing a cigarette' is identical to a hunger for food, although one will not satisfy the other. Like hunger, there is no physical pain and the feeling is so imperceptible that we are not even aware of it between cigarettes. It's only if we want to light up and aren't allowed to do so that we become aware of any discomfort. But when we do light up we feel satisfied.

It is this similarity to eating which helps to fool smokers

into believing that they receive some genuine pleasure. Some smokers find it very difficult to grasp that there is no pleasure or crutch whatsoever to smoking. Some argue: 'How can you say there is no crutch? You tell me when I light up that I'll feel less nervous than before.'

Although eating and smoking appear to be very similar, in fact they are exact opposites:

1. You eat to survive and to prolong your life, whereas smoking shortens your life.
2. Food does genuinely taste good, and eating is a genuinely pleasant experience that we can enjoy throughout our lives, whereas smoking involves breathing foul and poisonous fumes into your lungs.
3. Eating doesn't create hunger and genuinely relieves it, whereas the first cigarette starts the craving for nicotine and each subsequent one, far from relieving it, ensures that you suffer it for the rest of life.

This is an opportune moment to dispel another common myth about smoking – that smoking is a habit. Is eating a habit? If you think so, try breaking it completely. No, to describe eating as a habit would be the same as describing breathing as a habit. Both are essential for survival. It is true that different people are in the habit of satisfying their hunger at different times and with varying types of food. But eating itself is not a habit. Neither is smoking. The only reason any smoker lights a cigarette is to try to end the empty, insecure feeling that the previous cigarette created. It is true that different smokers are in the habit of trying to relieve their withdrawal pangs at different times but smoking itself is not a habit.

Society frequently refers to the smoking habit and in this book, for convenience, I sometimes also refer to the 'habit'. However, be constantly aware that smoking is not habit, on the contrary it is no more nor less than DRUG ADDICTION!

When we start to smoke we have to force ourselves to learn to cope with it. Before we know it, we are not only buying them regularly but we *have* to have them. If we don't, panic sets in, and as we go through life we tend to smoke more and more.

This is because, as with all drugs, the body develops a resistance to the effects of nicotine as it builds up a tolerance to it and so our intake tends to increase. After quite a short period of smoking the cigarette ceases to relieve completely the withdrawal pangs that it creates, so that when you light up a cigarette you feel better than you did a moment before, but you are in fact more nervous and less relaxed than you would be as a non-smoker, even when you are actually smoking the cigarette. The practice is even more ridiculous than wearing tight shoes for the relief of removing them because as you go through life an increasing amount of the discomfort remains even when the shoes are removed.

The position is even worse because, once the cigarette is extinguished, the nicotine rapidly begins to leave the body, which explains why, in stressful situations, the smoker tends to chain smoke.

As I said, the 'habit' doesn't exist. The real reason why every smoker goes on smoking is because of that little monster that feels like it's inside his stomach. Every now and again he has to feed it. The smoker himself will decide when he does that, and it tends to be on four types of occasion or a combination of them.

They are:

What magic drug can suddenly reverse the very effect it had twenty minutes before? If you think about it, what other types of occasion are there in our lives; apart from sleep? The truth is that smoking neither relieves boredom and stress nor promotes concentration and relaxation. It is all just illusion.

Apart from being a drug, nicotine is also a powerful poison and is used in insecticides (look it up in your dictionary). The nicotine content of just one cigarette, if injected directly into a vein, would kill you. In fact, tobacco contains many poisons, including carbon monoxide, and the tobacco plant is the same genus as 'deadly nightshade'.

In case you have visions of switching to a pipe or to cigars, I should make it quite clear that the content of this book applies to all tobacco and any product containing nicotine, including nicotine gum, patches, tabs, nasal sprays, lozenges, inhalators and Snus (orally taken tobacco common in Scandinavia).

The human body is the most sophisticated object on our planet. No species, even the lowest amoeba or worm, can survive without knowing the difference between food and poison.

Through a process of natural selection over thousands of years, our minds and bodies have developed techniques for distinguishing between food and poison and fail-safe methods for rejecting the latter.

All human beings are averse to the smell and taste of tobacco until they become hooked. If any animal or child inhales cigarette smoke before it becomes hooked, it will cough and splutter.

When we smoked our first cigarette, inhaling resulted in a coughing fit, or if we smoked too many the first time, we experienced a dizzy feeling or actual physical sickness. It was our body telling us, 'YOU ARE FEEDING ME POISON. STOP DOING IT.' This is the stage that often decides whether we become smokers or not. It is a fallacy that physically weak and mentally weak-willed people become smokers. The lucky ones are those who find that first cigarette repulsive; physically their lungs cannot cope with it, and they are cured for life. Or, alternatively, they are not mentally prepared to go through the severe learning process of trying to inhale without coughing.

To me this is the most tragic part of this whole business. How hard we worked to become hooked, and this is why it is difficult to stop teenagers. Because they are still learning to smoke, because they still find cigarettes distasteful, they believe they can stop whenever they want to. Why do they not learn from us? Then again, why did we not learn from our parents?

Many smokers believe they enjoy the taste and smell of the tobacco. It's an illusion. What we are actually doing when we learn to smoke is teaching our bodies to become immune to the bad smell and taste in order to get our fix. Heroin addicts believe they enjoy injecting themselves, but they don't. The withdrawal pangs from heroin are relatively severe, and all they are really enjoying is relieving those pangs.

The smoker teaches himself to shut his mind to the bad

taste and smell to get his 'fix'. Ask a smoker who believes he smokes only because he enjoys the taste and smell of tobacco, 'If you cannot get your normal brand of cigarette and can only obtain a brand you find distasteful, do you stop smoking?' No way. A smoker will smoke old rope rather than abstain, and it doesn't matter if you switch to roll-ups, mentholated cigarettes, cigars or a pipe; to begin with they taste awful but if you persevere, you will learn to like them. Smokers will even try to keep smoking during colds, flus, sore throats, bronchitis and emphysema.

Enjoyment has nothing to do with it. If it did, no one would smoke more than one cigarette. There are even thousands of ex-smokers hooked on that filthy nicotine chewing gum that doctors prescribe, and many of them are still smoking.

During consultations at my clinics some smokers find it alarming to realize they are drug addicts and think it will make it even more difficult to stop. In fact, it is all good news for two important reasons:

1. The reason why most of us carry on smoking is because, although we know the disadvantages outweigh the advantages, we believe that there is something in the cigarette that we actually enjoy or that it is some sort of prop. We feel that after we stop smoking there will be a void, that certain situations in our life will never be quite the same. This is an illusion. The fact is the cigarette gives nothing; it only takes away and then partially restores to create the illusion. I will explain this in more detail in a later chapter.
2. Although it is the world's most powerful drug because of the speed with which you become hooked, you are never badly hooked. Because it is a quick-acting drug it takes only three weeks for 99 per cent of the nicotine to leave

your body, and the actual withdrawal pangs are so mild that most smokers have lived and died without ever realizing that they have suffered them.

You will quite rightly ask why it is that many smokers find it so difficult to stop, go through months of torture and spend the rest of their lives pining for a cigarette at odd times. The answer is the second reason why we smoke – the brainwashing. The chemical addiction is easy to deal with.

Most smokers go all night without a cigarette. The withdrawal pangs do not even wake them up.

Many smokers will actually leave the bedroom before they light that first cigarette; many will have breakfast first, many will wait until just before they go into their workplace. They can suffer ten hours' withdrawal pangs, and it doesn't bother them, but if they went ten hours during the day without a cigarette, they'd be tearing their hair out.

Many smokers will buy a new car nowadays and refrain from smoking in it. Many will visit theatres, supermarkets, churches, etc, and not being able to smoke doesn't bother them. Even when nationwide smoking bans have been introduced there have been no riots. Smokers are almost pleased for someone or something to force them to stop smoking.

Nowadays many smokers will automatically refrain from smoking in the home of, or merely in the company of non-smokers with little discomfort to themselves. In fact, most smokers have extended periods during which they abstain without effort. Even in my case I would quite happily relax all evening without a cigarette. In the later years as a smoker I actually used to look forward to the evenings when I could stop choking myself (what a ridiculous 'habit').

The chemical addiction is easy to cope with, even when

you are still addicted, and there are thousands of smokers who remain casual smokers all their lives. They are just as heavily addicted as the heavy smoker. There are even heavy smokers who have kicked the 'habit' but will have an occasional cigar, and that keeps them addicted and they eventually end up back at square one.

As I say, the actual nicotine addiction is not the main problem. It just acts like a catalyst to keep our minds confused over the real problem: the brainwashing.

It may be of consolation to lifelong and heavy smokers to know that it is just as easy for them to stop as casual smokers. In a peculiar way, it is easier. The further you go along with the 'habit', the more it drags you down and the greater the gain when you stop.

It may be of further consolation for you to know that the rumours that occasionally circulate (e.g. 'It takes seven years for the "gunge" to leave your body' or 'Every cigarette you smoke takes five minutes off your life') are untrue.

Do not think the bad effects of smoking are exaggerated. If anything, they are sadly understated, but the truth is the 'five minutes' rule is obviously an estimation and applies only if you contract one of the killer diseases or just 'gunge' yourself to a standstill.

In fact, the 'gunge' never leaves your body completely. If there are smokers about, it is in the atmosphere, and even non-smokers acquire a small percentage. However, these bodies of ours are incredible machines and have enormous powers of recovery, providing you haven't already triggered off one of the irreversible diseases. If you stop now, your body will recover within a matter of a few weeks, almost as if you had never been a smoker.

As I have said, it is never too late to stop. I have helped

to cure many smokers in their fifties and sixties and even a few in their seventies and eighties. A 91-year-old woman attended my clinic with her 66-year-old son. When I asked her why she had decided to stop smoking, she replied, 'To set an example for him.' She contacted me six months later saying she felt like a young girl again.

The further it drags you down, the greater the relief. When I finally stopped I went straight from a hundred a day to ZERO, and didn't have one bad pang. In fact, it was actually enjoyable, even during the withdrawal period.

But we *must* remove the brainwashing.

7 Brainwashing and the Sleeping Partner

How or why do we start smoking in the first place? To understand this fully you need to examine the powerful effect of the subconscious mind or, as I call it, the 'sleeping partner'.

We all tend to think we are intelligent, dominant human beings determining our paths through life. In fact, 99 per cent of our make-up is moulded. We are a product of the society that we are brought up in – the sort of clothes we wear, the houses we live in, our basic life patterns, even those matters on which we tend to differ, e.g. political leanings. It's no coincidence that in the UK Labour supporters tend to come from the working classes and Conservatives from the middle and upper classes. The subconscious is an extremely powerful influence in our lives, and even in matters of fact rather than opinion millions of people can be deluded. Before Columbus sailed around the world the majority of people were certain it was flat. Today we know it's spherical. If I wrote a dozen books trying to persuade you that it was flat, I could not do it, yet how many of us have been into space to see the sphere? Even if you have flown or sailed around the world, how do you know that you were not travelling in a circle above a flat surface?

Advertising and marketing men know well the power of suggestion over the subconscious mind, hence the large posters the smoker used to be hit with as he drove around, the adverts that used to be in every magazine. You think they were a waste of money? That they did not persuade you to buy cigarettes? You are wrong! The tobacco industry still uses this advertising in countries where it is allowed to because they know it works. Indeed in the countries where cigarette advertising is banned, the industry still finds ways of getting its message across via photo shoots of glamorous models in fashion magazines and product placement in Hollywood movies and regular TV programmes. Try it out for yourself. Next time you go into a pub or restaurant on a cold day and your companion asks you what you are having to drink, instead of saying, 'A brandy' (or whatever), embellish it with 'Do you know what I would really enjoy today? That marvellous warm glow of a brandy.' You will find that even people who dislike brandy may join you.

From our earliest years our subconscious minds are bombarded daily with information telling us that cigarettes relax us and give us confidence and courage and that the most precious thing on this earth is a cigarette. You think I exaggerate? Whenever you see a cartoon or film or play in which people are about to be executed or shot, what is their last request? That's right, a cigarette. The impact of this does not register on our conscious minds, but the sleeping partner has time to absorb it. What the message is really saying is, 'The most precious thing on this earth, my last thought and action, will be the smoking of a cigarette.' In every war film the injured man is given a cigarette.

You think that things have changed recently? No, our children are still being bombarded by such images. As recently as 2006, research indicated that the frequency of smoking characters appearing in Hollywood movies had returned to the levels prevalent in the 1950s. Do you think this is accidental? Cigarette advertising is supposed to be banned on television nowadays, yet during peak viewing hours smoking is still portrayed as normal. Formula One motor racing still manages to avoid the ban on advertising in many ways. These images in sport and among film and TV personalities betray the most sinister trend of all: the link with sporting occasions and the jet set. Formula One racing cars used to be modelled and even named after cigarette brand names – or is it the other way round? How my admiration goes out to the advertisers of the small cigar, not for their motives but for the brilliance of that old campaign, whereby a man is about to face death or disaster as his balloon is on fire and about to crash, or the sidecar of his motor bike is about to crash into a river, or he's Columbus and his ship is about to go over the edge of the world. Not a word is spoken. Soft music plays. He lights up a cigar, a look of sheer bliss covers his face. The conscious mind may not have realized that the smoker was even watching the advert, but the 'sleeping partner' was patiently digesting the obvious implications. It is still going on to this day.

True, there is publicity the other way – the cancer scares, the legs being amputated, the bad-breath campaigns – but these do not actually stop people smoking. Logically they should, but the fact is they do not. They do not even prevent youngsters from starting. All the years that I remained a smoker I honestly believed that, had I known of the links between lung cancer and cigarette smoking, I would never have become a smoker. The truth is that it doesn't make the slightest bit of difference. The trap is the same today as when

Sir Walter Raleigh fell into it. All the anti-smoking campaigns just help to add to the confusion. Even the products themselves, those lovely shining packets that lure you into trying their contents, contain a deadly warning on their fronts. What smoker ever reads it, let alone brings himself to face the implications of it?

I believe that a leading cigarette manufacturer actually used to use the Government health warning to sell its products. Many of the scenes in its advertising used to include frightening images such as sharks, chainsaws, spiders, dragonflies and the Venus flytrap. The health warning is now so large and bold that the smoker cannot avoid it, however hard he tries. The pang of fear that the smoker suffers promotes an association of ideas with the glossy gold or purple packet.

Ironically, the most powerful force in this brainwashing is the smoker himself. It is a fallacy that smokers are weak-willed and physically weak specimens. You have to be physically strong in order to cope with the poison.

This is one of the reasons why smokers refuse to accept the overwhelming statistics that prove that smoking cripples your health. Everyone knows of an Uncle Fred who smoked forty a day, never had a day's illness in his life, and lived to eighty. They refuse even to consider the hundreds of other smokers who are cut down in their prime or the fact that Uncle Fred might still be alive if he hadn't been a smoker.

If you do a small survey among your friends and colleagues, you will find that most smokers are, in fact, strong-willed people. They tend to be self-employed, business executives or in certain specialized professions, such as doctors, lawyers, policemen, teachers, salesmen, nurses, secretaries, housewives with children, etc – in other words, anybody leading a stressful existence. The main delusion of smokers is that smoking relieves stress and tends to be associated with the dominant type, the type that takes on responsibility and stress, and, of course, that is the type that we admire and therefore tend to copy. Another group that tends to get hooked are people in monotonous jobs because the other main reason for smoking is boredom. However, the idea that smoking relieves boredom is also an illusion, I'm afraid.

The extent of the brainwashing is quite incredible. As a society we get all uptight about crack or heroin addiction, yet actual deaths from these drugs number in the thousands each year in the UK.

There is another drug, nicotine, on which over 60 per cent of us became hooked at some time in our lives and the majority spend the rest of their lives paying for it through the nose. Most of their spare money goes on cigarettes and hundreds of thousands of people have their lives ruined every year because they became hooked. It is the Number 1 killer in society, including road accidents, fires, etc.

Why is it that we regard crack or heroin addiction as such great evils, while taking the drug that we spend most of our money on and is actually killing us, we regarded until just a few years ago as a perfectly acceptable social habit? In recent years it has been revealed as a killer and become considered antisocial, but it's still legal and on sale in glossy packets in every newsagent, supermarket, off-licence and petrol station. The biggest vested interest is our own Government. In the UK the Government makes more than £8,000,000,000 per year out of smokers, and the tobacco companies spend over £100,000,000 per year in promotion alone in spite of the advertising bans.

You need to start building up a resistance to this brainwashing, just as if you were buying a car from a second-hand dealer. You would be nodding politely but you would not believe a word the man was saying.

Start looking behind these glossy packets at the filth and poison beneath. Do not be fooled by the cut-glass ashtrays or the gold lighters or the millions who have been conned. Start asking yourself:

Why am I doing it?

Do I really need to?

NO, OF COURSE YOU DON'T.

I find this brainwashing the most difficult aspect of smoking to explain. Why is it that an otherwise rational, intelligent human being becomes a complete imbecile about his own addiction? It pains me to confess that out of the millions of people that I have assisted in kicking smoking, I was the biggest idiot of all.

Not only did I reach a hundred a day myself, but my father was a heavy smoker. He was a strong man, cut down in his prime due to smoking. I can remember watching him when I was a boy; he would be coughing and spluttering in the mornings. I could see he wasn't enjoying it and it was so obvious to me that something evil had got possession of him. I can remember saying to my mother, 'Don't ever let me become a smoker.'

At the age of fifteen I was a physical-fitness fanatic. Sport was my life and I was full of courage and confidence. If anybody had said to me in those days that I would end up smoking a hundred cigarettes a day, I would have gambled my lifetime's earnings that it would not happen, and I would have given any odds that had been asked.

At the age of forty I was a physical and mental cigarette junky. I had reached the stage where I couldn't carry out the most mundane physical or mental act without first lighting up. With most smokers the triggers are the normal stresses of life, like answering the telephone or socializing. I couldn't even change a television programme or a light bulb without lighting up.

I knew it was killing me. There was no way I could kid myself otherwise. But why I couldn't see what it was doing to me mentally I cannot understand. It was almost jumping up and biting me on the nose. The ridiculous thing is that most smokers suffer the delusion at some time in their life that they enjoy a cigarette. I never suffered that delusion. I smoked because I thought it helped me to concentrate and because it helped my nerves. Now I am a non-smoker, the most difficult part is trying to believe that those days actually happened. It's like awakening from a nightmare, and that is about the size of it. Nicotine is a drug, and your senses are drugged – your taste buds, your sense of smell. The worst aspect of smoking isn't the injury to your health or pocket, it is the warping of the mind. You search for any plausible excuse to go on smoking.

I remember at one stage switching to a pipe, after a failed attempt to kick cigarettes, in the belief that it was less harmful and would cut down my intake.

Some of those pipe tobaccos are absolutely foul. The aroma can be pleasant but, to start with, they are awful to smoke. I can remember that for about three months the tip of my tongue was as sore as a boil. A liquid brown goo collects in the bottom of the bowl of the pipe. Occasionally you unwittingly bring the bowl above the horizontal and before you realize it you have swallowed a mouthful of the filthy stuff. The result is usually to throw up immediately, no matter what company you are in.

It took me three months to learn to cope with the pipe,

but what I cannot understand is why I didn't sit down sometime during that three months and ask myself why I was subjecting myself to the torture.

Of course, once they learn to cope with the pipe, no one appears more contented than pipe smokers. Most of them are convinced that they smoke because they enjoy the pipe. But why did they have to work so hard to learn to like it when they were perfectly happy without it?

The answer is that once you have become addicted to nicotine, the brainwashing is increased. Your subconscious mind knows that the little monster has to be fed, and you block everything else from your mind. As I have already stated, it is fear that keeps people smoking, the fear of that empty, insecure feeling that you get when you stop supplying the nicotine. Because you are not aware of it doesn't mean it isn't there. You don't have to understand it any more than a cat needs to understand where the under-floor hot-water pipes are. It just knows that if it sits in a certain place it gets the feeling of warmth.

It is the brainwashing that is the main difficulty in giving up smoking. The brainwashing of our upbringing in society reinforced with the brainwashing from our own addiction and, most powerful of all, the brainwashing of our friends, relatives and colleagues.

Did you notice that up to now I've frequently referred to 'giving up' smoking? I used the expression at the beginning of the previous paragraph. This is a classic example of the brainwashing. The expression implies a genuine sacrifice. The beautiful truth is that there is absolutely nothing to give up. On the contrary, you will be freeing yourself from a terrible disease and achieving marvellous positive gains. We are going to start removing this brainwashing now. From this point on, no longer will we refer to 'giving up', but to stopping, quitting or the true position: ESCAPING!

The only thing that persuades us to smoke in the first place is all the other people doing it. We feel we are missing out. We work so hard to become hooked, yet nobody ever finds out what they have been missing. But every time we see another smoker he reassures us that there must be something in it, otherwise he wouldn't be doing it. Even when he has quit, the ex-smoker feels he is being deprived when a smoker lights up at a party or other social function. He feels safe. He can have just one. And, before he knows it, he is hooked again.

This brainwashing is very powerful and you need to be aware of its effects. I remember as a youngster the Paul Temple detective series that was a very popular radio programme. One of the series was dealing with addiction to marijuana, commonly known as 'pot' or 'grass'. Unbeknown to the smoker, wicked men were selling cigarettes that contained 'pot'. There were no harmful effects. People merely became addicted and had to go on buying the cigarettes. (During my consultations literally hundreds of smokers have admitted to trying 'pot'. None of them said they became hooked on it.) I was about seven years old when I listened to this programme. It was my first knowledge of drug addiction. The concept of addiction, being compelled to go on taking the drug, filled me with horror, and even to this day, in spite of the fact that I am fairly convinced that 'pot' is not addictive, I would not dare take one puff of marijuana. How ironic that I should have ended up a junky on the world's Number 1 addictive drug. If only Paul Temple had warned me about the cigarette itself. How ironic too that over forty years later mankind spends thousands of pounds on cancer research, yet millions are spent persuading healthy teenagers to become hooked on the filthy weed, our own government having the largest vested interest.

We are about to remove the brainwashing. It is not the non-smoker who is being deprived but the poor smoker who is forfeiting a lifetime of:

HEALTH
ENERGY
WEALTH
PEACE OF MIND
CONFIDENCE
COURAGE
SELF-RESPECT
HAPPINESS
FREEDOM

And what does he gain from these considerable sacrifices?

ABSOLUTELY NOTHING – except the illusion of trying to get back to the state of peace, tranquillity and confidence that the non-smoker enjoys all the time.

8 Relieving Withdrawal Pangs

As I explained earlier, smokers think they smoke for enjoyment, relaxation or some sort of boost. In fact, this is an illusion. The actual reason is the relief of withdrawal pangs.

In the early days we use the cigarette as a social prop. We can take it or leave it. However, the subtle chain has started. Our subconscious mind begins to learn that a cigarette taken at certain times appears to be pleasurable.

The more we become hooked on the drug, the greater the need to relieve the withdrawal pangs and the further the cigarette drags you down, the more you are fooled into believing it is doing the opposite. It all happens so slowly, so gradually, you are not even aware of it. Each day you feel no different from the day before. Most smokers don't even realize they are hooked until they actually try to stop, and even then many won't admit to it. A few stalwarts just keep their heads in the sand all their lives, trying to convince themselves and other people that they enjoy it.

I have had the following conversation with hundreds of teenagers.

ME: You realize that nicotine is a drug and that the only reason why you are smoking is that you cannot stop.

T: Nonsense! I enjoy it. If I didn't, I would stop.

ME: Just stop for a week to prove to me you can if you want to.

T: No need. I enjoy it. If I wanted to stop, I would.

ME: Just stop for a week to prove to yourself you are not hooked.

T: What's the point? I enjoy it.

As already stated, smokers tend to relieve their withdrawal pangs at times of stress, boredom, concentration, relaxation or a combination of these. This point is explained in greater detail in the next few chapters.

9 Stress

I am referring not only to the great tragedies of life but also to the minor stresses, the socializing, the telephone call, the anxieties of the housewife with noisy young children and so on.

Let us use the telephone conversation as an example. For most people the telephone is slightly stressful, particularly for the businessman. Most calls aren't from satisfied customers or your boss congratulating you. There's usually some sort of aggro – something going wrong or somebody making demands. At that time the smoker, if he isn't already doing so, will light up a cigarette if he can. He doesn't know why he does this, but he does know that for some reason it appears to help.

What has actually happened is this. Without being conscious of it, he has already been suffering aggravation (i.e. the withdrawal pangs). By partially relieving that aggravation at the same time as normal stress, the total stress is reduced and the smoker gets a boost. At this point the boost is not, in fact, an illusion. The smoker will feel better than before he lit the cigarette. However, even when smoking that cigarette the smoker is more tense than if he were a non-smoker because the more you go into the drug, the more it knocks you down and the less it restores you when you smoke.

I promised no shock treatment. In the example I am about to give, I am not trying to shock you, I am merely emphasizing that cigarettes destroy your nerves rather than relax them.

Try to imagine getting to the stage where a doctor tells you that unless you stop smoking he is going to have to remove your legs. Just for a moment pause and try to visualize life without your legs. Try to imagine the frame of mind of a man who, issued with that warning, actually continues smoking and then has his legs removed.

I used to hear stories like that and dismissed them as cranky. In fact, I used to wish a doctor would tell me that; then I would have stopped. Yet I was already fully expecting any day to have a brain haemorrhage, and lose not only my legs but my life. I didn't think of myself as a crank, just a heavy smoker.

Such stories are not cranky. That is what this awful drug does to you. As you go through life it systematically takes away your nerve and courage. The more it takes our courage away, the more you are deluded into believing the cigarette is doing the opposite. We have all heard of the panic that overtakes smokers when they are out late at night and in fear of running out of cigarettes. Non-smokers do not suffer from it. The cigarette causes that feeling. At the same time, as you go through life the cigarette not only destroys your nerves but is a powerful poison, progressively destroying your physical health. By the time the smoker reaches the stage at which it is killing him, he believes the cigarette is his courage and cannot face life without it.

Get it clear in your mind: the cigarette is not calming your nerves, it is slowly but steadily destroying them. One of the great gains of getting free is the return of your confidence and self-assurance.

10
Boredom

If you are already smoking at this moment, you will probably have forgotten about it until I reminded you.

Another fallacy about smoking is that cigarettes relieve boredom. Boredom is a frame of mind. When you smoke a cigarette your mind isn't saying: 'I'm smoking a cigarette. I'm smoking a cigarette.' The only time that happens is when you have been deprived for a long time or are trying to cut down, or during those first few cigarettes after a failed attempt to stop.

The true situation is this: when you are addicted to nicotine and are not smoking, there is something missing. If you have something to occupy your mind that isn't stressful, you can go for long periods without being bothered by the absence of the drug. However, when you are bored there's nothing to take your mind off it, so you feed the monster. When you are indulging yourself (i.e. not trying to stop or cut down), even lighting up becomes subconscious. Even pipe smokers and roll-your-own smokers can perform this ritual automatically. If any smoker tries to remember the cigarettes he has smoked during the day, he can only remember a small proportion of them – e.g. the first of the day or the one after a meal.

The truth is that cigarettes tend to increase boredom indirectly because they make you feel lethargic, and instead of undertaking some energetic activity smokers tend to lounge around, bored, relieving their withdrawal pangs.

This is why countering the brainwashing is so important. Because it's a fact that smokers tend to smoke when they are bored and that we've been told since birth that smoking relieves boredom, it doesn't occur to us to question the fact. We've also been brainwashed into believing that chewing gum aids relaxation. It is a fact that when under stress people tend to grind their teeth. All chewing gum does is to give you a logical reason to grind your teeth. Next time you watch someone chewing gum, observe them closely and ask yourself whether they looked relaxed or tense. Observe smokers who are smoking because they are bored. They still look bored. The cigarette doesn't relieve the boredom.

As an ex-chain smoker I can assure you that there are no more boring activities in life than lighting up one filthy cigarette after another, day in day out, year in year out.

Concentration

Cigarettes do not help concentration. That is just another illusion.

When you are trying to concentrate, you automatically try to avoid distractions like feeling cold or hot. The smoker is already suffering: that little monster wants his fix. So when he wants to concentrate he doesn't even have to think about it. He automatically lights up, partially ending the craving, gets on with the matter in hand and has already forgotten that he is smoking.

Cigarettes do not help concentration. They help to ruin it because after a while, even while smoking a cigarette, the smoker's withdrawal pangs cease to be completely relieved. The smoker then increases his intake, and the problem then increases.

Concentration is also affected adversely for another reason. The progressive blocking up of the arteries and veins with poisons starves the brain of oxygen. In fact, your concentration and inspiration will be greatly improved as this process is reversed.

It was the concentration aspect that prevented me from succeeding when using the willpower method. I could put up with the irritability and bad temper, but when I really needed to concentrate on something difficult, I had to have that cigarette. I can well remember the panic I felt when I discovered that I was not allowed to smoke during my accountancy exams. I was already a chain-smoker and convinced that I would not be able to concentrate for three hours without a cigarette. But I passed the exams, and I can't even remember thinking about smoking at the time, so, when it came to the crunch, it obviously didn't bother me.

The loss of concentration that smokers suffer when they try to stop smoking is not, in fact, due to the physical withdrawal from nicotine. When you are a smoker, you have mental blocks. When you have one, what do you do? If you are not already smoking one, you light a cigarette. That doesn't cure the mental block, so then what do you do? You do what you have to do: you get on with it, just as non-smokers do. When you are a smoker nothing gets blamed on the cigarette. Smokers never have smoking coughs; they just have permanent colds. The moment you stop smoking, everything that goes wrong in your life is blamed on the fact that you've stopped smoking. Now when you have a mental block, instead of just getting on with it you start to say, 'If only I could light up now, it would solve my problem.' You then start to question your decision to quit smoking.

If you believe that smoking is a genuine aid to concentration, then worrying about it will guarantee that you won't be able to concentrate. It's the doubting, not the physical withdrawal pangs, that causes the problem. Always remember: it is smokers who suffer withdrawal pangs and not non-smokers.

When I extinguished my last cigarette I went overnight from a hundred a day to zero without any apparent loss of concentration.

Relaxation

Most smokers think that a cigarette helps to relax them. The truth is that nicotine is a chemical stimulant. If you take your pulse and then smoke two consecutive cigarettes, there will be a marked increase in your pulse rate.

One of the favourite cigarettes for most smokers is the one after a meal. A meal is a time of day when we stop working; we sit down and relax, relieve our hunger and thirst and are then completely satisfied. However, the poor smoker cannot relax, as he has another hunger to satisfy. He thinks of the cigarette as the icing on the cake, but it is the little monster that needs feeding.

The truth is that the nicotine addict can never be completely relaxed, and as you go through life it gets worse.

The most unrelaxed people on this planet aren't non-smokers but fifty-year-old business executives who chain-smoke, are permanently coughing and spluttering, have high blood pressure and are constantly irritable. By this stage cigarettes cease even partially to relieve the symptoms they have created.

I can remember when I was a young accountant, bringing up a family. One of my children would do something wrong and I would lose my temper to an extent that was out of all proportion to what he had done. I really believed that I had an evil demon in my make-up. I now know that I had, however it wasn't some inherent flaw in my character, but the little nicotine monster that was creating the problem. During those times I thought I had all the problems in the world, but when I look back on my life I wonder where all the great stress was. In everything else in my life I was in control. The one thing that controlled me was the cigarette. The sad thing is that even today I can't convince my children that it was the smoking that caused me to be so irritable. Every time they hear a smoker trying to justify his addiction, the message is 'Oh, they calm me. They help me to relax.'

I remember when the adoption authorities first threatened to prevent smokers from adopting children. A man rang up a radio show on the subject, irate. He said, 'You are completely wrong. I can remember when I was a child, if I had a contentious matter to raise with my mother, I would wait until she lit a cigarette because she was more relaxed then.' Why couldn't he talk to his mother when she wasn't smoking a cigarette? Why are smokers so unrelaxed when they are not smoking, even after a meal at a restaurant? Why are non-smokers completely relaxed then? Why are smokers not able to relax without a cigarette? The next time you are in a supermarket and you see a young mother or father screaming at a child, just watch them leave. The first thing they will do is light a cigarette. Start watching smokers, particularly when they are not allowed to smoke. You'll find that they have their hands near their mouths, or they are twiddling their thumbs, or tapping their feet, or fiddling with their hair, or clenching their jaw. Smokers aren't relaxed. They've forgotten what it feels like to be completely relaxed. That's one of the many joys you have to come.

The whole business of smoking can be likened to a fly being caught in a pitcher plant. To begin with, the fly is attracted by the nectar. At some imperceptible stage the plant begins to eat the fly. Isn't it time you climbed out of that plant?

13

Combination Cigarettes

No, a combination cigarette is not when you are smoking two or more at the same time. When that happens, you begin to wonder why you were smoking the first one. I once burnt the back of my hand trying to put a cigarette in my mouth when there was already one there. Actually, it is not quite as stupid as you think. As I have already said, eventually the cigarette ceases to relieve the withdrawal pangs, and even when you are smoking the cigarette there is still something missing. This is the terrible frustration of the chain-smoker. Whenever you need the boost, you are already smoking, and this is why heavy smokers often turn to drink or other drugs. But I digress.

A combination cigarette is one occasioned by two or more of our usual reasons for smoking, e.g. social functions, parties, weddings. These are examples of occasions that are both stressful and relaxing. This might at first appear to be a contradiction, but it isn't. Any form of socializing can be stressful, even with friends, and at the same time you want to be enjoying yourself and be completely relaxed.

There are situations where all four reasons are present at one and the same time. Driving can be one of these. If you are leaving a tense situation, like a visit to the dentist or the doctor, you can now relax. At the same time driving always involves an element of stress. Your life is at stake. You are also having to concentrate. You may not be aware of the last two factors, but the fact that they are subconscious doesn't mean they aren't there. And if you are stuck in a traffic jam, or have a long motorway drive, you may also be bored.

Another classic example is a game of cards. If it's a game like bridge or poker, you have to concentrate. If you are losing more than you can afford, it is stressful. If you have long periods of not getting a decent hand, it can be boring. And, while all this is going on, you are at leisure; you are supposed to be relaxing. During a game of cards, no matter how slight the withdrawal pangs are, all smokers will be chain-smoking, even otherwise casual smokers. The ashtrays will fill and overflow in no time. There'll be a constant fall-out cloud above head height. If you were to tap any of the smokers on the shoulder and ask him if he was enjoying it, the answer would be, 'You have got to be joking.' It is often after nights like these, when we wake up with a throat like a cesspit, that we decide to stop smoking.

These combination cigarettes are often special ones, the ones that we think we'll miss most when we are contemplating stopping smoking. We think that life will never be quite as enjoyable again. In fact, it is the same principle at work: these cigarettes simply provide relief from withdrawal pangs, and at certain times we have greater need to relieve them than at others.

Let us make it quite clear. It is not the cigarette that is special; it is the occasion. Once we have removed the need for the cigarette, such occasions will become more enjoyable and the stressful situations less stressful. This will be explained in greater detail in the next chapter.

14

What am I Giving up?

ABSOLUTELY NOTHING! The thing that makes it difficult for us to quit is fear. The fear that we are being deprived of our pleasure or prop. The fear that certain pleasant situations will never be quite the same again. The fear of being unable to cope with stressful situations.

In other words, the effect of brainwashing is to delude us into believing that there is a weakness in us, or something inherent in the cigarette that we need, and that when we stop smoking there will be a void.

Get it clear in your mind: CIGARETTES DO NOT FILL A VOID. THEY CREATE IT!

These bodies of ours are the most sophisticated objects on this planet. Whether you believe in a creator, a process of natural selection or a combination of both, whatever being or system devised these bodies of ours, it is a thousand times more effective than man! Man cannot create the smallest living cell, let alone the miracle of eyesight, reproduction, our circulatory system or our brains. If the creator or process had intended us to smoke, we would have been provided with some filter device to keep the poisons out of our bodies and some sort of chimney.

Our bodies are, in fact, provided with fail-safe warning

devices in the form of the cough, dizziness, sickness, etc, and we ignore these at our peril.

The beautiful truth is – there is nothing to give up. Once you purge that little monster from your body and the brain-washing from your mind, you will neither want cigarettes nor need them.

Cigarettes do not improve meals. They ruin them. They destroy your sense of taste and smell. Observe smokers in a restaurant, going outside for cigarettes between courses. They're not enjoying the meal. In fact, they can't wait for the meal to be over as it's interfering with their smoking. In the days when smokers could light up in restaurants, many of them did in spite of the fact that they knew it caused offence to non-smokers. It's not that smokers are generally inconsiderate people, it's just that they are miserable without the cigarette. They are between the devil and the deep blue sea. They either have to abstain and be miserable because they cannot smoke, or smoke and be miserable because they are offending other people, feel guilty and despise themselves for it.

Watch smokers at an official function or in a restaurant. Many of them develop weak bladders and have to sneak off for a crafty puff. That is when you see smoking for the true addiction that it is. Smokers do not smoke because they enjoy it. They do it because they are miserable without it.

Because many of us start smoking on social occasions when we are young and shy, we acquire the belief that we cannot enjoy social occasions without a cigarette. This is nonsense. Tobacco takes away your confidence. The greatest evidence of the fear that cigarettes instil in smokers is their effect on women. Practically all women are fastidious about their personal appearance. They wouldn't dream of appearing at a social function not immaculately turned out and smelling beautiful. Yet knowing that their breath smells like a stale ashtray and their clothes stink does not seem to deter them in the least. I know that it *bothers* them greatly – many hate the smell of their own hair and clothes – yet it doesn't *deter* them. Such is the fear that this awful drug instils in the smoker.

Cigarettes do not help social occasions; they destroy them. Having to hold a drink in one hand and a cigarette in the other, trying to dispose of the ash and the continual chain of dog ends, trying not to breathe smoke and fumes into the face of the person you are conversing with, wondering whether they can smell your breath or see the stains on your teeth.

Not only is there nothing to give up, but there are marvellous positive gains. When smokers contemplate quitting smoking they tend to concentrate on health, money and social stigma. These are obviously valid and important issues, but I personally believe the greatest gains from stopping are psychological, and for varying reasons they include:

1. The return of your confidence and courage
2. Freedom from the slavery
3. Not to have to go through life suffering the awful black shadows at the back of your mind, knowing you are being despised by half of the population and, worst of all, despising yourself

Not only is life better as a non-smoker but it is infinitely more enjoyable. I do not only mean you will be healthier and wealthier. I mean you will be happier and enjoy life far more.

The marvellous gains from being a non-smoker are discussed in the next few chapters.

Some smokers find it difficult to appreciate the concept of the 'void', and the following analogy may assist you.

Imagine having a cold sore on your face. I've got this marvellous ointment. I say to you, 'Try this stuff.' You rub the ointment on, and the sore disappears immediately. A week later it reappears. You ask, 'Do you have any more of that ointment?' I say, 'Keep the tube. You might need it again.' You apply the ointment. Hey presto, the sore disappears again. Every time the sore returns, it gets larger and more painful and the interval gets shorter and shorter. Eventually the sore covers your whole face and is excruciatingly painful. It is now returning every half hour. You know that the ointment will remove it temporarily, but you are very worried. Will the sore eventually spread over your whole body? Will the interval disappear completely? You go to your doctor. He can't cure it. You try other things, but nothing helps except this marvellous ointment.

By now you are completely dependent on the ointment. You never go out without ensuring that you have a tube of the ointment with you. If you go abroad you make sure that you take several tubes with you. Now, in addition to your worries about your health, I'm charging you £200 per tube. You have no choice but to pay me.

You then read in the medical column of your newspaper that this isn't happening just to you; many other people have been suffering from the same problem. In fact, pharmacists have discovered that the ointment doesn't actually cure the sore. All that it does is to take the sore beneath the surface of the skin. It is the ointment that has caused the sore to grow. All you have to do to get rid of the sore is to stop using the ointment. The sore will eventually disappear in due course.

Would you continue to use the ointment?

Would it take willpower not to use the ointment? If you didn't believe the article, there might be a few days of apprehension, but once you realized that the sore was beginning to get better, the need or desire to use the ointment would go.

Would you be miserable? Of course you wouldn't. You had an awful problem, which you thought was insoluble. Now you've found the solution. Even if it took a year for that sore to disappear completely, each day, as it improved, you'd think, 'Isn't it marvellous? I'm not going to die.'

This was the magic that happened to me when I extinguished that final cigarette. Let me make one point quite clear in the analogy of the sore and the ointment. The sore isn't lung cancer, or arterial sclerosis, or emphysema, or angina, or chronic asthma, or bronchitis, or coronary heart disease. They are all in addition to the sore. It isn't the thousands of pounds that we burn, or the lifetime of bad breath and stained teeth, the lethargy, the wheezing and coughing, the years we spend choking ourselves and wishing we didn't, the times when we are being punished because we are not allowed to smoke. It isn't the lifetime of being despised by other people, or, worst of all, despising yourself. These are all in addition to the sore. The sore is what makes us close our minds to all these things. It's that panic feeling of 'I want a cigarette.' Non-smokers don't suffer from that feeling. The worst thing we ever suffer from is fear, and the greatest gain you will receive is to be rid of that fear.

It was as if a great mist had suddenly lifted from my mind. I could see so clearly that the panic feeling of wanting a cigarette wasn't some sort of weakness in me, or some magic quality in the cigarette. It was caused by the first cigarette; and each subsequent one, far from relieving the feeling, was causing it. At the same time I could see that all these other 'happy' smokers were going through the same nightmare that I was. Not as bad as mine, but all putting up phoney arguments to try to justify their stupidity.

IT'S SO NICE TO BE FREE!

15
Self-imposed Slavery

Usually when smokers try to stop the main reasons are health, money and social stigma. Part of the brainwashing of this awful drug is the sheer slavery.

Man fought hard to abolish slavery, and yet the smoker spends his life suffering self-imposed slavery. He seems to be oblivious to the fact that, when he is allowed to smoke, he wishes that he were a non-smoker. With most of the cigarettes we smoke in our lives, not only do we not enjoy them but we aren't even aware that we are smoking them. It is only after a period of abstinence that we actually suffer the delusion of enjoying a cigarette (e.g. the first in the morning, the one after a meal, etc).

The only time that the cigarette becomes precious is when we are trying to cut down or abstain, or when society tries to force us not to smoke with smoking bans.

The confirmed smoker should bear in mind that this trend will get worse and worse. Today it is all public places. Tomorrow it will be your own car, home and garden.

Gone are the days when the smoker could enter a friend's or stranger's house and say, 'Do you mind if I smoke?' Nowadays the poor smoker, on entering a strange house, will search desperately for an ashtray and hope to find dog ends in it. If there is no ashtray, he will generally try to last out, and if he cannot, he will ask for permission to smoke and is likely to be told: 'Smoke if you have to,' or 'Well, we would rather you didn't. The smell seems to linger on.'

The poor smoker, who was already feeling wretched, wants the ground to open up and swallow him.

I remember during my smoking days, every time I went to church, it was an ordeal. Even during my own daughter's wedding, when I should have been standing there a proud father, what was I doing? I was thinking, 'Let's get on with it, so that we can get outside and have a drag.'

It will help you to observe smokers on these occasions. They huddle together. There is never just one packet. There are twenty packets being thrust about, and the conversation is always the same.

'Do you smoke?'

'Yes, but have one of mine.'

'I will have one of yours later.'

They light up and take a deep drag, thinking, 'Aren't we lucky? We have got our little reward. The poor non-smoker hasn't got a reward.'

The 'poor' non-smoker doesn't need a reward. We were not designed to go through life systematically poisoning our own bodies. The pathetic thing is that even when smoking a cigarette, the smoker doesn't achieve the feeling of peace, confidence and tranquillity that the non-smoker has experienced for the whole of his non-smoking life. The non-smoker isn't sitting in the church feeling agitated and wishing his life away. He can enjoy the whole of his life.

I can also remember playing indoor bowls in the winter and pretending to have a weak bladder in order to nip off for a puff. No, this wasn't a fourteen-year-old schoolboy but a forty-year-old chartered accountant. How pathetic. And even when I was back playing the game I wasn't enjoying it. I was looking forward to the finish so that I could smoke again, yet this was supposed to be my way of relaxing and enjoying my favourite hobby.

To me one of the tremendous joys of being a non-smoker is to be freed from that slavery, to be able to enjoy the whole of my life and not spend half of it craving a cigarette and then, when I light up, wishing I didn't have to do it.

Smokers should bear in mind that when they are in the houses of non-smokers or even in the company of non-smokers, it is not the self-righteous non-smoker who is depriving them but the 'little monster'.

16

I'll Save £x a Week

I cannot repeat too often that it is brainwashing that makes it difficult to stop smoking, and the more brainwashing we can dispel before we start, the easier you will find it to achieve your goal.

Occasionally I get into arguments with people whom I call confirmed smokers. By my definition a confirmed smoker is somebody who can afford it, doesn't believe it injures his health and isn't worried about the social stigma. (There are not many about nowadays.)

If he is a young man, I say to him, 'I cannot believe you are not worried about the money you are spending.'

Usually his eyes light up. If I had attacked him on health grounds or on the social stigma, he would feel at a disadvantage, but on money – 'Oh, I can afford it. It is only £x per week and I think it is worth it. It is my only vice or pleasure,' etc.

If he is a twenty-per-day smoker I say to him, 'I still cannot believe you are not worried about the money. You are going to spend over £75,000 in your lifetime. What are you doing with that money? You are not even setting light to it or throwing it away. You are actually using that money to ruin your physical health, to destroy your nerves and confidence, to suffer a lifetime of slavery, a lifetime of bad breath and stained teeth. Surely that must worry you?'

It is apparent at this point, particularly with young smokers, that they have never considered it a lifetime expense. For most smokers the price of a packet is bad enough. Occasionally we work out what we spend in a week, and that is alarming. Very occasionally (and only when we think about stopping) we estimate what we spend in a year and that is frightening, but over a lifetime – it is unthinkable.

However, because it is an argument the confirmed smoker will say, 'I can afford it. It is only so much a week.' He does an 'encyclopaedia salesman' on himself.

I then say, 'I will make you an offer you cannot refuse. You pay me £2,000 now, and I will provide you with free cigarettes for the rest of your life.'

If I were offering to take over a £75,000 mortgage for £2,000, the smoker would have my signature on a piece of paper before I could move, and yet not one confirmed smoker (and please bear in mind I am not now talking to someone like yourself who plans to stop, I am talking to someone who claims to have no intention of stopping) has ever taken me up on that offer. Why not?

Often at this point at my clinics, a smoker will say, 'Look, I am not really worried about the money aspect.' If you are thinking along these lines, ask yourself why you are not worried. Why in other aspects of life will you go to a great deal of trouble to save a few pounds here and there and yet spend thousands of pounds poisoning yourself and hang the expense?

The answer to these questions is this. Every other decision that you make in your life will be the result of an analytical process of weighing up the pros and cons and arriving at a rational answer. It may be the wrong answer, but at least it will be the result of rational deduction. Whenever any smoker weighs up the pros and cons of smoking, the answer is a dozen times over: 'STOP SMOKING! YOU ARE A MUG!' Therefore all smokers are smoking not because they want to or because they decided to but because they think they cannot stop. They have to brainwash themselves. They have to keep their heads in the sand.

The strange thing is smokers will arrange pacts among themselves to try to quit, such as 'First one to give in pays the other £50,' yet the thousands of pounds that they would save by stopping doesn't seem to affect them. This is because they are still thinking with the brainwashed mind of the smoker.

Just take the sand out of your eyes for a moment. Smoking is a chain reaction and a chain for life. If you do not break that chain, you will remain a smoker for the rest of your life. Now estimate how much you think you will spend on smoking for the rest of your life. The amount will obviously vary with each individual, but for the purpose of this exercise let us assume it is another £40,000.

You will shortly be making the decision to smoke your final cigarette (not yet, please – remember the initial instructions). All you have to do to remain a non-smoker is not to fall for the trap again. That is, do not smoke that first cigarette. If you do, that one cigarette will cost you £40,000.

If you think this is a trick way of looking at it, you are still kidding yourself. Just work out how much money you would have saved if you hadn't smoked your first cigarette.

If you see the argument as factual, ask yourself how you would feel if a cheque for £40,000 from a competition you'd won were to arrive in your post tomorrow. You'd be dancing with delight! So start dancing! You are about to start receiving that bonus, and that's just one of the several marvellous gains you are about to receive.

During the withdrawal period you may be tempted to have just one final cigarette. It will help you to resist the temptation if you remind yourself it will cost you £40,000 (or whatever your estimate is)!

I've been making that offer to confirmed smokers on television and radio programmes for years. I still find it incredible that not one confirmed smoker has ever taken up my offer. There are members of my golf club whom I taunt every time I hear them complain about an increase in tobacco prices. In fact, I'm frightened that if I goad them too much, one of them will take me up on it. I'd lose a fortune if he did.

If you are in the company of happy, cheerful smokers who tell you how much they enjoy it, just tell them that you know an idiot who, if they pay him a year's smoking money in advance, will provide them with free cigarettes for the rest of their lives. Perhaps you can find me someone who will take up the offer?

Health

This is the area where the brainwashing is the greatest. Smokers think they are aware of the health risks. They are not.

Even in my case, when I was expecting my head to explode any moment and honestly believed I was prepared to accept the consequences, I was still kidding myself.

If in those days I had taken a cigarette out of the packet and a red bleeper started to sound, followed by a warning voice saying, 'OK, Allen, this is the one! This is your warning. Up to now you have got away with it, but if you smoke another cigarette your head will explode,' do you think I would have lit that cigarette?

If you are in doubt about the answer, just try walking up to a main road with busy traffic, stand on the kerb with your eyes closed and try to imagine you have the choice of either stopping smoking or walking blindfolded across the road before taking your next cigarette.

There is no doubt what your choice would be. I had been doing what every smoker does all his smoking life: closing my mind and keeping my head in the sand, hoping that I would wake up one morning and just not want to smoke any more. Smokers cannot allow themselves to think of the health risks. If they do, even the illusion of enjoying the 'habit' goes.

This explains why the shock treatment used by the media on National No-Smoking Days is so ineffective. It is only non-smokers who can bring themselves to watch. It also explains why smokers, recalling Uncle Fred who smoked forty a day and lived until he was eighty, will ignore the thousands of people who are brought down in their prime because of this poisonous weed.

About six times a week I have the following conversation with smokers (usually the younger ones):

ME: Why do you want to stop?

SMOKER: I can't afford it.

ME: Aren't you worried about the health risks?

SMOKER: No. I could step under a bus tomorrow.

ME: Would you deliberately step under a bus?

SMOKER: Of course not.

ME: Do you not bother to look left and right when you cross the road?

SMOKER: Of course I do.

Exactly. The smoker goes to a lot of trouble not to step under a bus, and the odds are hundreds of thousands to one against it happening. Yet the smoker risks the near certainty of being crippled by the weed and appears to be completely oblivious to the risks. Such is the power of the brainwashing.

I remember one famous British golfer who wouldn't go on the American circuit because he was afraid of flying. Yet he would chain-smoke round the golf course. Isn't it strange that, if we felt there was the slightest fault in an aeroplane, we wouldn't go up in it, even though the risks are hundreds of thousands to one against death, yet we take a one-in-two certainty with the cigarette and are apparently oblivious to it. And what does the smoker get out of it?

ABSOLUTELY NOTHING!

Another common myth about smoking is the smoker's cough. Many of the young people who attend my clinics are not worried about their health because they do not cough. The true facts are just the reverse. A cough is one of nature's fail-safe methods of dispelling foreign matter from the lungs. The cough itself is not a disease; it is just a symptom. When smokers cough it is because their lungs are trying to dispel cancer-triggering tars and poisons. When they do not cough those tars and poisons remain in their lungs, and that is when they cause cancer. Smokers tend to avoid exercise and get into the habit of shallow breathing in order not to cough. I used to believe that my permanent smoker's cough would kill me. By expelling much of the filth from my lungs, it possibly saved my life.

Just think of it this way. If you had a nice car and allowed it to rust without doing anything about it, that would be pretty stupid, as it would soon be a heap of rust and would not carry you about. However, that would not be the end of the world; it is only a question of money and you could always buy a new one. Your body is the vehicle that carries you through life. We all say that our health is our most valued asset. How true that is, as sick millionaires will tell you. Most of us can look back at some illness or accident in our lives when we prayed to get better. (HOW SOON WE FORGET.) By being a smoker you are not only letting rust get in and doing nothing about it; you are systematically destroying the vehicle you need to go through life, and you only get one.

Wise up. You don't have to do it, and remember: it is doing ABSOLUTELY NOTHING FOR YOU.

Just for a moment take your head out of the sand and ask yourself, if you knew for certain that the next cigarette would be the one to trigger off cancer in your body, whether you would actually smoke it. Forget the disease (it is difficult to imagine it), but imagine you have to go to hospital to suffer those awful tests and terrible treatments, etc. Now you are not planning the rest of your life. You are planning your death. What is going to happen to your family and loved ones, your plans and dreams?

I often see the people that it happens to. They didn't think it would happen to them either, and the worst thing about it isn't the disease itself but the knowledge that they have brought it on themselves. All our lives as smokers we are saying, 'I'll stop tomorrow.' Try to imagine how those people feel who 'hit the button'. For them the brainwashing is ended. They then see the 'habit' as it really is and spend the remainder of their lives thinking, 'Why did I kid myself I needed to smoke? If only I had the chance to go back!'

Stop kidding yourself. You have the chance. It's a chain reaction. If you smoke the next cigarette, it will lead to the next one and the next. It's already happening to you.

At the beginning of the book I promised you no shock treatment. If you have already decided you are going to stop smoking, this isn't shock treatment for you. If you are still in doubt, skip the remainder of this chapter and come back to it when you have read the rest of the book.

Volumes of statistics have already been written about the damage that cigarettes can cause to the smoker's health. The trouble is that until the smoker decides to stop he doesn't want to know. Even the government health warning is a waste of time because the smoker puts blinkers on, and if he inadvertently reads it, the first thing he does is light up a cigarette.

Smokers tend to think of the health hazards as a hit-and-miss affair, like stepping on a mine. Get it into your head: it is already happening. Every time you puff on a cigarette you are breathing cancer-triggering tars into your lungs, and cancer is by no means the worst of the killer diseases that cigarettes cause or contribute to. They are also a powerful contributory cause of heart disease, arteriosclerosis, emphysema, angina, thrombosis, chronic bronchitis and asthma.

While I was still smoking, I'd never heard of arteriosclerosis or emphysema. I knew the permanent wheezing and coughing and the ever-increasing asthma and bronchitis attacks were a direct result of my smoking. But though they caused me discomfort there was no real pain and I could handle the discomfort.

I confess that the thought of contracting lung cancer terrified me, which is probably why I just blocked it from my mind. It's amazing how the fear of the horrendous health risks attached to smoking are overshadowed by the fear of stopping. It's not so much that the latter is a greater fear, but that if we quit today the fear is immediate, whereas the fear of contracting lung cancer is a fear of the future. Why look on the black side? Perhaps it won't happen. I'm bound to have quit by then anyway.

We tend to think of smoking as a tug of war. On one side fear: it's unhealthy, expensive, filthy and enslaving. On the other side the plusses: it's my pleasure, my friend, my crutch. It never seems to occur to us that this side is also fear. It's not so much that we enjoy them, but that we tend to be miserable without them.

Think of heroin addicts deprived of their heroin: the abject misery they go through. Now picture their utter joy when they are allowed to plunge a needle into their veins and end that terrible craving. Try to imagine how anyone could actually believe they get pleasure from sticking a hypodermic syringe into a vein.

Non-heroin addicts don't suffer that panic feeling. Heroin doesn't relieve the feeling, on the contrary, it causes it. Non-smokers don't feel miserable if they are not allowed to smoke after a meal. It's only smokers that suffer that feeling. Nicotine doesn't relieve it, on the contrary it causes it.

The fear of contracting lung cancer didn't make me quit because I believed it was rather like walking through a minefield. If you got away with it – fine. If you were unlucky you stepped on a mine. You knew the risks you were taking and if you were prepared to take the risk, what had it to do with anyone else?

So if a non-smoker ever tried to make me aware of those risks, I would use the typical evasive tactics that all addicts invariably adopt.

'You have to die of something.'

Of course you do, but is that a logical reason for deliberately shortening your life?

'Quality of life is more important than longevity.'

Exactly, but you are surely not suggesting that the quality of life of an alcoholic or a heroin addict is greater than that of someone that isn't addicted to alcohol or heroin? Do you really believe that the quality of a smoker's life is better than a non-smoker's? Surely the smoker loses on both counts – his life is both shorter and more miserable.

'My lungs probably suffer more damage from car exhausts than from smoking.'

Even if that were true, is that a logical reason for punishing your lungs further? Can you possibly conceive of anyone being stupid enough to actually put their mouth over an exhaust pipe and deliberately inhale those fumes into their lungs?

THAT'S WHAT SMOKERS EFFECTIVELY DO!

Think of that next time you watch a poor smoker inhale deeply on one of those 'precious' cigarettes!

I can understand why the congestion and the risks of contracting lung cancer didn't help me to quit. I could cope with the former and block my mind to the latter. As you are already aware, my method is not to frighten you into quitting, but the complete opposite – to make you realize just how more enjoyable your life will be when you have escaped.

However, I do believe that if I could have seen what was happening inside my body, this would have helped me to quit. Now I'm not referring to the shock technique of showing a smoker the colour of a smoker's lungs. It was obvious to me from my nicotine-stained teeth and fingers that my lungs weren't a pretty sight. Provided they kept functioning, they were less embarrassment than my teeth and fingers – at least nobody could see my lungs.

What I am referring to is the progressive gunging-up of our arteries and veins and the gradual starving of every muscle and organ of our bodies of oxygen and nutrients and replacing them with poisons and carbon monoxide (not just from car exhausts but also from smoking).

Like the majority of motorists, I don't like the thought of dirty oil or a dirty filter in my car engine. Could you imagine buying a brand new Rolls-Royce and never changing the oil or the oil filter? That's what we effectively do to our bodies when we become smokers.

Many doctors are now relating all sorts of diseases to smoking, including diabetes, cervical cancer and breast cancer. This is no surprise to me. The tobacco industry has laboured the fact that the medical profession has never scientifically proved that smoking was the direct cause of lung cancer.

The statistical evidence is so overwhelming as not to need proof. No one ever scientifically proved to me exactly why, when I bang my thumb with a hammer, it hurts. I soon got the message.

I must emphasize that I am not a doctor, but just like the hammer and the thumb, it soon became obvious to me that my congestion, my permanent cough, my frequent asthma and bronchial attacks were directly related to my smoking. However, I truly believe that the greatest hazard that smoking causes to our health is the gradual and progressive deterioration of our immune system caused by this gunging-up process.

All plants and animals on this planet are subjected to a lifetime of attack from germs, viruses, parasites, etc. The most powerful defence we have against disease is our immune system. We all suffer infections and diseases throughout our lives. I believe we are all threatened by cancer in its early forms at some point during our lives. However, I do not believe that the human body was designed to be diseased, and if you are strong and healthy, your immune system will fight and defeat these attacks. How can your immune system work effectively when you are starving every muscle and organ of oxygen and nutrients and replacing them with carbon monoxide and poisons? It's not so much that smoking causes these other disease, it works rather like AIDs, it gradually destroys your immune system.

Several of the adverse effects that smoking had on my health, some of which I had been suffering from for years, did not become apparent to me until many years after I had stopped smoking.

While I was busy despising those idiots and cranks who would rather lose their legs than quit smoking, it didn't even occur to me that I was already suffering from arteriosclerosis myself. My almost permanently grey complexion I attributed to my natural colouring or to lack of exercise. It never occurred to me that it was really due to the blocking up of my capillaries. I had varicose veins in my thirties, which have miraculously disappeared since I stopped smoking. I reached the stage about five years before I stopped when every night I would have this weird sensation in my legs. It wasn't a sharp pain or like pins and needles, just a sort of restless feeling. I would get Joyce to massage my legs every night. It didn't occur to me until at least a year after I had stopped that I no longer needed the massage.

About two years before I quit, I would occasionally get violent pains in my chest, which I feared must be lung cancer but now assume to have been angina. I haven't had a single attack since I quit.

When I was a child I would bleed profusely from cuts. This frightened me. No one explained to me that bleeding was in fact a natural and essential healing process and that the blood would clot when its healing purpose was completed. I suspected that I was a haemophiliac and feared that I might bleed to death. Later in life I would sustain quite deep cuts yet hardly bleed at all. The browny-red gunge would ooze from the cut. The colour worried me. I knew that blood was meant to be bright red and I assumed that I had some sort of blood disease. However I was pleased about the consistency, which meant that I no longer bled profusely. Not until after I had stopped smoking did I learn that smoking coagulates the blood and that the brownish colour was due to lack of oxygen. I was ignorant of the effect at the time, but in hindsight, it was this effect that smoking was having on my health that most fills me with horror. When I think of my poor heart trying to pump that gunge around restricted blood vessels, day in and day out, without missing a single beat, I find it a miracle that I didn't suffer a stroke or a heart attack. It made me realize, not how fragile our bodies are, but how strong and ingenious that incredible machine is!

I had liver spots on my hands in my forties. In case you don't know, liver spots are those brown or white spots that very old people have on their face and hands. I tried to ignore them, assuming that they were due to early senility caused by the hectic lifestyle that I had led. It was five years after I had quit that a smoker at my clinic in Raynes Park remarked that when he had stopped previously, his liver spots disappeared. I had forgotten about mine, and to my amazement, they too had disappeared.

As long as I can remember, I had spots flashing in front of my eyes if ever I stood up too quickly, particularly if I were in a bath. I would feel dizzy, as if I were about to black out. I never related this to smoking. In fact I was convinced that it was quite normal and that everyone else had a similar reaction. Not until only five years ago, when an ex-smoker told me that he no longer had that sensation did it occur to me that I no longer had it either.

You might conclude that I am somewhat of a hypochondriac. I believe that I was when I was a smoker. One of the great evils about smoking is that it fools us into believing that nicotine gives us courage, when in fact it gradually and imperceptibly dissipates it. I was shocked when I heard my father say that he had no wish to live to be fifty. Little did I realize that twenty years later I would have exactly the same lack of *joie de vivre*. You might conclude that this chapter has been one of necessary, or unnecessary, doom and gloom. I promise you it is the complete opposite. I used to fear death when I was a child. I used to believe that smoking removed that fear. Perhaps it did. If so, it replaced it with something infinitely worse: A FEAR OF LIVING!

Now my fear of dying has returned. It does not bother me. I realize that it only exists because I now enjoy life so much. I don't brood over my fear of dying any more than I did when I was a child. I'm far too busy living my life to the full. The odds are against my living to a hundred, but I'll try to. I'll also try to enjoy every precious moment!

There were two other advantages on the health side that never occurred to me until I had stopped smoking. One was that I used to have repetitive nightmares every night. I would dream that I was being chased. I can only assume that these nightmares were the result of the body being deprived of nicotine throughout the night and the insecure feeling that would result. Now the only nightmare that I have is that I occasionally dream I am smoking again. This is quite a common dream among ex-smokers. Some worry that it means that they are still subconsciously pining for a cigarette. Don't worry about it. The fact that it was a nightmare means that you are very pleased not to be a smoker. There is that twilight zone after any nightmare when you wake up and are not sure whether it is a genuine catastrophe, but isn't it marvellous when you realize that it was only a dream?

When I described being chased every night in a dream, I originally typed 'chaste'. Perhaps this was just a 'Freudian slip', but it does give me a convenient lead into the second advantage. At my clinics, when covering the effect that smoking has on concentration, we sometimes say: 'Which organ in your body has the greatest need of a good supply of blood?' The stupid grins, usually on the faces of the men, would indicate that they had missed the point. However, they were absolutely right. Being a somewhat shy Englishman, I find the subject rather embarrassing, and I have no intention of doing a miniature 'Kinsey' report by going into detail about the adverse effect that smoking had on my own sexual activity and enjoyment, or that of other ex-smokers with whom I have discussed the subject. Again, I was not aware of this effect until some time after I had stopped smoking and had attributed my sexual prowess and activity, or rather lack of it, to advancing years.

However, if you watch natural-science films, you will be aware that the first rule of nature is survival and that the second rule is survival of the species, or reproduction. Nature ensures that reproduction does not take place unless the partners feel physically healthy and know that they have secured a safe home, territory, supply of food and a suitable mate. Man's ingenuity has enabled him to bend these rules somewhat; however, I know for a fact that smoking can lead to impotence. I can also assure you that when you feel fit and healthy, you'll enjoy sex much more and more often.

Smokers also suffer the illusion that the ill-effects of smoking are overstated. The reverse is the case. There is no doubt that cigarettes are the Number 1 cause of death in society. The trouble is that in many cases where cigarettes cause the death or are a contributory factor, it is not blamed on cigarettes in the statistics.

It has been estimated that 44 per cent of household fires are caused by cigarettes, and I wonder how many road accidents have been caused by cigarettes during that split second when you take your eye off the road to light up.

I am normally a careful driver, but the nearest I came to death (except from smoking itself) was when trying to roll a cigarette while driving, and I hate to think of the number of times I coughed a cigarette out of my mouth while driving – it always seemed to end up between the seats. I am sure many other smoking drivers have had the experience of trying to locate the burning cigarette with one hand while trying to drive with the other.

The effect of the brainwashing is that we tend to think like the man who, having fallen off a 100-storey building, is heard to say, as he passes the fiftieth floor, 'So far, so good!' We think that as we have got away with it so far, one more cigarette won't make the difference.

Try to see it another way: the 'habit' is a continuous chain for life, each cigarette creating the need for the next. When you start the 'habit' you light a fuse. The trouble is, YOU DON'T KNOW HOW LONG THE FUSE IS. Every time that you light a cigarette you are one step nearer to the bomb exploding. HOW WILL YOU KNOW IF IT'S THE NEXT ONE?

Energy

Most smokers are aware of the effect that this progressive process of gunging-up and starvation of oxygen and nutrients has on their lungs. However, they are not so aware of the effect it has on their energy level.

One of the subtleties of the smoking trap is that the effects it has on us, both physical and mental, happen so gradually and imperceptibly that we are not aware of them and regard them as normal.

It is very similar to the effects of bad eating habits. The pot-belly appears so gradually that it causes us no alarm. We look at people who are grossly overweight and wonder how they could possibly have allowed themselves to reach that stage.

But supposing it happened overnight. You went to bed weighing ten stone, trim, rippling with muscles and not an ounce of fat on your body. You awoke weighing thirteen stone, fat, bloated and pot-bellied. Instead of waking up feeling fully rested and full of energy, you wake up feeling miserable, lethargic and you can hardly open your eyes. You would be panic-stricken, wondering what awful disease you had contracted overnight. Yet the disease is exactly the same. The fact that it took you twenty years to reach that state is irrelevant.

So it is with smoking. If I could immediately transfer you into your mind and body to give you a direct comparison on how you would feel having stopped smoking for just three weeks, that is all I would need to do to persuade you to quit. You would think: 'Will I really feel this good?' Or what it really amounts to: 'Have I really sunk that low?' I emphasize that I don't just mean how you would feel healthier and have more energy, but how you would feel more confident and relaxed and better able to concentrate.

As a teenager, I can remember rushing around just for the hell of it. For thirty-odd years, I was permanently tired and lethargic. I used to struggle to wake up at nine o'clock in the morning. After my evening meal I would lie on a settee watching television and nod off after five minutes. Because my father used to be the same, I thought this behaviour was normal. I believed that energy was the exclusive prerogative of children and teenagers, and that old age began in the early twenties.

Shortly after I extinguished my final cigarette, I was relieved that the congestion and the coughing disappeared, and I haven't had an asthma or bronchitis attack since. However, something truly marvellous and unexpected also happened. I started waking at seven o'clock in the morning feeling completely rested and full of energy, actually wanting to exercise, jog and swim. At forty-eight I couldn't run a step or swim a stroke. My sporting activities were confined to such dynamic pursuits as green bowling, affectionately referred to as the old man's game, and golf, for which I had to use a motorized buggy. At the age of sixty-four I was jogging two to three miles daily, exercising for half an hour and swimming twenty lengths a day. It's great to have energy, and when you feel physically and mentally strong, it feels great to be alive.

The problem is that when you quit smoking, the return of your physical and mental health is also gradual. True it's nothing like as slow as the slide into the pit, and if you are going through the trauma of the willpower method of quitting, any health or financial gains will be obliterated by the depression you will be going through.

Unfortunately, I cannot immediately transfer you into your mind and body in three weeks' time. But you can! You know instinctively that what I am telling you is correct. All you need to do is: USE YOUR IMAGINATION!

19 It Relaxes Me and Gives Me Confidence

This is the worst fallacy of all about smoking, and for me it ranks with the ending of the slavery, as one of the greatest benefits from quitting — not to have to go through life with the permanent feeling of insecurity that smokers suffer from.

Smokers find it very difficult to believe that the cigarette actually causes that insecure feeling you get when you are out late at night and running out of cigarettes. Non-smokers do not suffer from that feeling. It is the tobacco that causes it.

I only became aware of many of the advantages of stopping months afterwards, as a result of my consultations with other smokers.

For twenty-five years I refused to have a medical. If I wanted life assurance, I insisted on 'no medical' and paid higher premiums as a result. I hated visiting hospitals, doctors or dentists. I couldn't face the thought of getting old, pensions and so on.

None of these things did I relate to my smoking 'habit', but getting off it has been like awakening from a bad dream. Nowadays I look forward to each day. Of course, bad things happen in my life, and I am subject to the normal stresses and strains, but it is wonderful to have the confidence to cope with them, and extra health, energy and confidence make the good times more enjoyable too.

20
Those Sinister Black Shadows

Another of the great joys of quitting the weed is to be free of those sinister black shadows at the back of our minds.

All smokers know they are mugs and close their minds to the ill-effects of smoking. For most of our lives smoking is automatic, but the black shadows are always lurking in our subconscious minds, just beneath the surface.

There are several marvellous advantages to achieve from quitting smoking. Some of them I was consciously aware of throughout my smoking life, such as the health risks, the waste of money and the sheer stupidity of being a smoker. However, such was my fear of quitting, so obsessed was I with resisting all the attempts of do-gooders and anyone else who tried to persuade me to quit, that all my imagination and energy were directed to finding any flimsy excuse that would allow me to continue to smoke.

Amazingly, my most ingenious thoughts occurred when I was actually trying to quit. They were of course inspired by the fear and misery I suffered when attempting to quit by using willpower. No way could I block my mind from the health and financial aspects. But now that I am free it amazes me how I successfully blocked my mind from even more important advantages to be gained from quitting. I've already mentioned the sheer slavery – spending half our lives being allowed to smoke, doing it automatically and wishing we had never started, the other half feeling miserable and deprived because society won't allow us to smoke. In the last chapter I referred to the incredible joy of having energy again. But for me the greatest joy of being free was not the health, the money, the energy, or the ending of the slavery, it was the removal of those sinister black shadows, the removal of feeling despised by and feeling apologetic to non-smokers, and most of all to be able to respect yourself.

Most smokers aren't the weak-willed, spineless jellyfish that both society and themselves tend to believe. In every other aspect of my life I was in control. I loathed myself for being dependent on an evil weed that I knew was ruining my life. I cannot tell you of the utter joy of being free of those sinister black shadows, the dependency and the self-despising. I can't tell you how nice it is to be able to look at all other smokers, whether they be young, old, casual or heavy, not with a feeling of envy, but with a feeling of pity for them and elation for you that you are no longer the slave of that insidious weed.

The last two chapters have dealt with the considerable advantages of being a non-smoker. I feel it necessary to give a balanced account, so the next chapter lists the advantages of being a smoker.

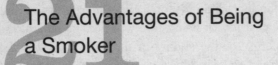

The Advantages of Being
a Smoker

22 The Willpower Method of Stopping

It is an accepted fact in our society that it is very difficult to stop smoking. Even books advising you how to do so usually start off by telling you how difficult it is. The truth is that it is ridiculously easy. Yes, I can understand you questioning that statement, but just consider it.

If your aim is to run a mile in under four minutes, that's difficult. You may have to undergo years of hard training, and even then you may be physically incapable of doing it. (Much of our achievement lies in the mind. Isn't it strange how difficult it was until Bannister actually did it but nowadays it's commonplace?)

However, in order to stop smoking all you have to do is not smoke any more. No one forces you to smoke (apart from yourself) and, unlike food or drink, you don't need it to survive. So if you want to stop doing it, why should it be difficult? In fact, it isn't. It is smokers who make it difficult by using the Willpower Method. I define the Willpower Method as any method that forces the smoker to feel he is making some sort of sacrifice. Let us just consider the Willpower Method.

We do not decide to become smokers. We merely experiment with the first few cigarettes and because they taste awful we are convinced that we can stop whenever we want to. In the main, we smoke those first few cigarettes only when we want to, and that is usually in the company of other smokers on social occasions.

Before we realize it, we are not only buying them regularly and smoking when we want to, we are smoking every day. Smoking has become a part of our lives. We ensure that we always have cigarettes on our person. We believe that social occasions and meals are improved by them and that they help to relieve stress. It doesn't seem to occur to us that the same cigarette out of the same packet will taste exactly the same after a meal as it does first thing in the morning. In fact smoking neither improves meals and social occasions nor does it relieve stress, it's just that smokers believe they can't enjoy a meal or handle stress without a cigarette.

It usually takes us a long time to realize that we are hooked because we suffer from the illusion that smokers smoke because they enjoy a cigarette, not because they have to have a cigarette. While we are not enjoying them (which we never do), we suffer from the illusion that we can stop whenever we want to.

Usually it is not until we actually try to stop that we realize a problem exists. The first attempts to stop are more often than not in the early days and are usually triggered off by shortage of money (boy meets girl and they are saving to set up home and do not want to waste money on cigarettes) or health (the teenager is still active in sport and finds he is short of breath). Whatever the reason, the smoker always waits for a stressful situation, whether it be health or money. As soon as he stops, the little monster needs feeding. The smoker then wants a cigarette, and because he cannot have one this makes him more distressed. The thing he usually takes to relieve stress is now not available, so he suffers a triple blow. The probable result after a period of torture is the compromise 'I'll cut down,' or 'I've picked the wrong time,' or 'I'll wait until the stress has gone from my life.' However, once the stress has gone, he has no need to stop and doesn't decide to do so again until the next stressful time. Of course, the time is never right because life for most people doesn't become less stressful; it becomes more so. We leave the protection of our parents and enter the world of setting up home, taking on mortgages, having children, more responsible jobs, etc. Of course, the smoker's life can never become less stressful because it is the cigarette that actually causes stress. As the smoker's rate of nicotine intake rises, the more distressed he becomes and the greater the illusion of his dependency becomes.

In fact, it is an illusion that life becomes more stressful, and it's the smoking itself, or a similar crutch, that creates the illusion. This will be discussed in greater detail in chapter 28.

After the initial failures the smoker usually relies on the possibility that one day he will wake up and just not want to smoke any more. This hope is usually kindled by the stories that he has heard about other ex-smokers (e.g. 'I had a bout of flu and afterwards I didn't want to smoke any more').

Don't kid yourself. I have probed all of these rumours, and they are never quite as simple as they appear. Usually the smoker has already been preparing himself to stop and merely used the flu as a springboard. I spent thirty-odd years waiting to wake up one morning wanting never to smoke again. Whenever I had a bad chest I would look forward to its ending because it was interfering with my smoking.

More often in the case of people who stop 'just like that' they have suffered a shock. Perhaps a close relative has died from a cigarette-related disease or they have had a scare themselves. It is so much easier to say, 'I just decided to stop one day. That's the sort of chap I am.' Stop kidding yourself! It won't happen unless you make it happen.

Let's consider in greater detail why the Willpower Method is so difficult. For most of our lives we adopt the head-in-the sand, 'I'll stop tomorrow' approach.

At odd times something will trigger off an attempt to stop. It may be concern about health, money, social stigma or we have been going through a particularly heavy bout of choking and realize that we don't actually enjoy it.

Whatever the reason, we take our head out of the sand and start weighing up the pros and cons of smoking. We then find out what we have known all our lives: on a rational assessment the conclusion is, a dozen times over, STOP SMOKING.

If you were to sit down and give points out of ten to all the advantages of stopping and do a similar exercise with the advantages of smoking, the total point count for stopping would far outweigh the disadvantages.

However, although the smoker knows that he will be better off as a non-smoker, he does believe that he is making a sacrifice. Although it is an illusion, it is a *powerful* illusion. The smoker doesn't know why, but he believes that during the good times and the bad times of life the cigarette does appear to help.

Before he starts the attempt he has the brainwashing of our society, reinforced by the brainwashing of his own addiction. To these must be added the even more powerful brainwashing of 'how difficult it is to give up'.

He has heard stories of smokers who have stopped for many months and are still desperately craving a cigarette.

There are all the disgruntled stoppers (people who stop and then spend the rest of their lives bemoaning the fact that they'd love a cigarette). He has heard of smokers who have stopped for many years, apparently leading happy lives, but have one cigarette and are suddenly hooked again. Probably he also knows several smokers in the advanced stages of disease who are visibly destroying themselves and are clearly not enjoying cigarettes – yet they continue to smoke. Added to all this, he has probably already suffered one or more of these experiences himself.

So, instead of starting with the feeling 'Great! Have you heard the news? I haven't got to smoke any more,' he starts with a feeling of doom and gloom, as if he were trying to climb Everest, and he firmly believes that once the little monster has got his hooks into you, you are hooked for life. Many smokers even start the attempt by apologizing to their friends and relatives: 'Look, I am trying to give up smoking. I will probably be irritable during the next few weeks. Try to bear with me.' Most attempts are doomed before they start.

Let's assume that the smoker survives a few days without a cigarette. The congestion is rapidly disappearing from his lungs. He hasn't bought cigarettes and consequently has more money in his pocket. So the reasons why he decided to stop in the first place are rapidly disappearing from his thoughts. It is like seeing a bad road accident when you are driving. It slows you down for a while, but the next time you are late for an appointment you have forgotten all about it and your foot stamps on the throttle.

On the other side of the tug of war, that little monster inside your stomach hasn't had his fix. There is no physical pain; if you had the same feeling because of a cold, you wouldn't stop working or get depressed. You would laugh it off. All the smoker knows is that he wants a cigarette. Quite why it is so important to him he doesn't know. The little monster in the stomach then starts off the big monster in the mind, and now the person who a few hours or days earlier was listing all the reasons to stop is desperately searching for any excuse to start again. Now he is saying thinks like:

1. Life is too short. The bomb could go off. I could step under a bus tomorrow. I have left it too late. They tell you everything gives you cancer these days.
2. I have picked the wrong time. I should have waited until after Christmas/after my holidays/after this stressful event in my life.
3. I cannot concentrate. I am getting irritable and bad tempered. I cannot do my job properly. My family and friends won't love me. Let's face it, for everybody's sake I have got to start smoking again. I am a confirmed smoker and there is no way I will ever be happy again without a cigarette. (This one kept me smoking for thirty-three years).

At this stage the smoker usually gives in. He lights a cigarette and the schizophrenia increases. On the one hand there is the tremendous relief of ending the craving, when the little monster finally gets his fix; on the other hand, if he has survived a long time, the cigarette tastes awful and the smoker cannot understand why he is smoking it. This is why the smoker thinks he lacks willpower. In fact, it is not lack of willpower; all he has done is to change his mind and make a perfectly rational decision in the light of the latest information. What's the point of being healthy if you are miserable? What is the point of being rich if you are miserable? Absolutely none.

Far better to have a shorter enjoyable life than a lengthy miserable life.

Fortunately, that is not true – just the reverse. Life as a non-smoker is infinitely more enjoyable, but it was this delusion that kept me smoking for thirty-three years, and I must confess, if that were the true situation, I would still be smoking (correction – I wouldn't be here).

The misery that the smoker is suffering has nothing to do with withdrawal pangs. True, they trigger them off, but the actual agony is in the mind and it is caused by doubt and uncertainty. Because the smoker starts by feeling he is making a sacrifice, he begins to feel deprived – this is a form of stress. One of the times when his brain tells him, 'Have a cigarette,' is a time of stress. Therefore as soon as he stops, he wants a cigarette. But now he can't have one because he has stopped smoking. This makes him more depressed, which sets the trigger off again.

Another thing that makes it so difficult is the waiting for something to happen. If your objective is to pass a driving test, as soon as you have passed the test it is certain you have achieved your objective. Under the Willpower Method you say, 'If I can go long enough without a cigarette, the urge to smoke will eventually go.'

How do you know when you have achieved it? The answer is that you never do because you are waiting for something to happen and nothing else is going to happen. You stopped when you smoked that last cigarette, and what you are really doing now is waiting to see how long it will be before you give in.

As I said above, the agony that the smoker undergoes is mental, caused by the uncertainty. Although there is no physical pain, it still has a powerful effect. The smoker is miserable and feeling insecure. Far from forgetting about smoking his mind becomes obsessed with it.

There can be days or even weeks of black depression. His mind is obsessed with doubts and fears.

'How long will the craving last?'

'Will I ever be happy again?'

'Will I ever want to get up in the morning?'

'Will I ever enjoy a meal again?'

'How will I ever cope with stress in future?'

'Will I ever enjoy a social function again?'

The smoker is waiting for things to improve, but of course while he is still moping, the cigarette is becoming more precious.

In fact, something does happen, but the smoker isn't conscious of it. If he can survive three weeks without inhaling any nicotine at all, the physical craving for nicotine disappears. However, as stated before, the pangs of withdrawal from nicotine are so mild that the smoker isn't aware of them. But after about three weeks many smokers sense that they have 'kicked it'. They then light a cigarette to prove it, and it does just that. It tastes awful, but the ex-smoker has now supplied nicotine to the body, and as soon as he extinguishes that cigarette the nicotine starts to leave the body. There is now a little voice at the back of his mind saying, 'You want another one.' In fact, he had kicked it but now he has hooked himself again.

The smoker will not usually light another cigarette immediately. He thinks, 'I don't want to get hooked again.' So he allows a safe period to pass. It might be hours, days, even weeks. The ex-smoker can now say, 'Well, I didn't get hooked, so I can safely have another.' He has fallen into the same trap as he did in the first place and is already on the slippery slope.

Smokers who succeed under the Willpower Method tend to find it long and difficult because the main problem is the brainwashing, and long after the physical addiction has died the smoker is still moping about cigarettes. Eventually, if he can survive long enough, it begins to dawn on him that he is not going to give in. He stops moping and accepts that life goes on and is enjoyable without the cigarette.

Many smokers are succeeding with this method, but it is difficult and arduous, and there are many more failures than successes. Even those who do succeed go through the rest of their lives in a vulnerable state. They are left with a certain amount of the brainwashing and believe that during good and bad times the cigarette can give you a boost. (Most non-smokers also suffer from that illusion. They are subject to the brainwashing also but either find they cannot learn to 'enjoy' smoking or don't want the bad side, thank you very much.) This explains why many smokers who have stopped for long periods start smoking again.

Many ex-smokers will have the occasional cigar or cigarette either as a 'special treat' or to convince themselves how awful they are. It does exactly that, but as soon as they put it out the nicotine starts to leave and a little voice at the back of their mind is saying, 'You want another one.' If they light another one, it still tastes awful and they say, 'Marvellous! While I am not enjoying them I won't get hooked. After Christmas/the holiday/this trauma, I will stop.'

Too late. They are already hooked. The trap that they fell into in the first place has claimed its victim again.

As I keep saying, enjoyment doesn't come into it. It never did! If we smoked because we enjoyed it, nobody would ever smoke more than one cigarette. We assume we enjoy them only because we cannot believe we would be so stupid as to smoke if we didn't enjoy them. This is why so much of our smoking is subconscious. If, while smoking every cigarette, you were aware of the foul fumes going into your lungs and you had to say to yourself, 'This is going to cost £75,000 in my lifetime, and this cigarette might just be the one to trigger off cancer in my lungs,' even the illusion of enjoyment would go. When we try to block our minds to the bad side, we feel stupid. If we had to face up to it, that would be intolerable! If you watch smokers, particularly at social functions, you will see that they are happy only when they are not aware that they are smoking. Once they become aware of it, they tend to be uncomfortable and apologetic. We smoke to feed that little monster . . . and once you have purged the little monster from your body and the big monster from your brain, you will have neither need nor desire to smoke.

23

Beware of Cutting Down

Many smokers resort to cutting down either as a stepping stone towards stopping or as an attempt to control the little monster, and many doctors and advisers recommend cutting down as an aid.

Obviously, the less you smoke the better off you are, but, as a stepping stone to stopping, cutting down is fatal. It is our attempts to cut down that keep us trapped all our lives.

Usually cutting down follows failed attempts to stop. After a few hours or days of abstinence the smoker says to himself something like, 'I cannot face the thought of being without a cigarette, so from now on I will just smoke the special ones or I will cut down to ten a day. If I can get in the habit of smoking ten a day, I can either hold it there or cut down further.'

Certain terrible things now happen.

1. He has the worst of all worlds. He is still addicted to nicotine and is keeping the monster alive not only in his body but also in his mind.
2. He is now wishing his life away waiting for the next cigarette.
3. Prior to cutting down, whenever he wanted a cigarette he

lit one up and at least partially relieved his withdrawal pangs. Now, in addition to the normal stresses and strains of life, he is actually causing himself to suffer the withdrawal pangs from nicotine most of his life. So he is causing himself to be miserable and bad tempered.

4. While he was indulging himself, he didn't enjoy most of the cigarettes and he didn't realize he was smoking them. It was automatic. The only cigarettes that he imagined he enjoyed were after a period of abstinence (e.g. the first in the morning, the one after a meal, etc). Now that he waits an extra hour for each cigarette, he 'enjoys' every one. The longer he waits, the more enjoyable each cigarette appears to become because the 'enjoyment' in a cigarette isn't the cigarette itself; it's the ending of the agitation caused by the craving, whether it be the slight physical craving for nicotine or the mental moping. The longer you suffer, the more 'enjoyable' each cigarette becomes.

The main difficulty of stopping smoking is not the chemical addiction. That's easy. Smokers will go all night without a cigarette; the craving doesn't even wake them up. Many smokers will actually leave the bedroom before they light up. Many will actually have breakfast. Some will even wait until they arrive at work.

They will go ten hours without a cigarette and it doesn't bother them. If they went ten hours during the day without one, they would be tearing their hair out.

Many smokers will buy a new car and abstain from smoking in it. Smokers will visit supermarkets, theatres, doctors, hospitals, dentists and so on without undue inconvenience. Many smokers will abstain in the company of non-smokers. Even since the bans on smoking in public places there have been no riots. Smokers are almost pleased for someone to say they cannot smoke. In fact, smokers get a secret pleasure out of going long periods without a cigarette. It gives them the hope that maybe one day they will never want another one.

The real problem when stopping smoking is the brainwashing, the illusion that the cigarette is some sort of prop or reward and life will never be quite the same without it. Far from turning you off smoking, all cutting down does is to leave you feeling insecure and miserable and to convince you that the most precious thing on this earth is the next cigarette, that there is no way that you will ever he happy without one.

There is nothing more pathetic than the smoker who is trying to cut down. He suffers from the delusion that the less he smokes, the less he will want to smoke. In fact, the reverse is true. The less he smokes, the longer he suffers the withdrawal pangs; the more he thinks he enjoys the cigarette, the more distasteful they become. But that won't stop him smoking. Taste never, ever came into it. If smokers smoked because they enjoyed the taste, nobody would ever smoke more than one cigarette. You find that difficult to believe. OK, let's talk it out. Which is the worst-tasting cigarette? That's right, the first in the morning, the one that in winter sets us coughing and spluttering. Which is one of the most precious cigarettes for most smokers? That's right, the first cigarette in the morning! Now do you really believe you are smoking it to enjoy the taste and smell, or do you think a more rational explanation is that you are relieving nine hours' withdrawal pangs?

It is essential that we remove all the illusions about smoking before you extinguish that final cigarette. Unless you've removed the illusion that you enjoy the taste of certain cigarettes before you extinguish the final one, there is no way you can prove it afterwards without getting hooked again. So, unless you are already smoking one, light one up now. Inhale six deep lungfuls of that glorious tobacco and ask yourself what is so glorious about the taste. Perhaps you believe that it is only certain cigarettes that taste good, like the one after a meal. If so, why do you bother to smoke the others? Because you got into the habit of doing it? Now why would anyone get into the habit of smoking cigarettes that they find distasteful? And why should the same cigarette out of the same package taste different after a meal than it tastes first thing in the morning. Food doesn't taste different after a cigarette, so why should a cigarette taste different after food?

Don't just rely on me, check it out, smoke a cigarette consciously after a meal to prove that it tastes no different. The reason smokers believe that cigarettes taste better after a meal or at social occasions with alcohol, is because those are the times when both non-smokers and smokers are really happy, but a nicotine addict can never be really happy if that little nicotine monster remains unsatisfied. It's not so much that smokers enjoy the taste of tobacco after a meal, after all, we don't eat tobacco, where does taste come into it? It's just that they are miserable if they aren't allowed to relieve their withdrawal symptoms at those times. So the difference between smoking and not smoking is the difference between being happy and miserable. That's why the cigarette appears to taste better. Whereas smokers who light up first thing in the morning are miserable whether they are smoking or not.

Cutting down not only doesn't work but it is the worst form of torture. It doesn't work because initially the smoker hopes that by getting into the habit of smoking less and less, he will reduce his desire to smoke a cigarette. It is not a habit. It is an addiction, and the nature of any addiction is to want more and more, not less and less. Therefore in order to cut down, the smoker has to exercise willpower and discipline for the rest of his life.

The main problem of stopping smoking is not the chemical addiction to nicotine. That's easy to cope with. It is the mistaken belief that the cigarette gives you some pleasure. This mistaken belief is brought about initially by the brain-washing we receive before we start smoking, which is then reinforced by the actual addiction. All cutting down does is reinforce the fallacy further to the extent that smoking domi-nates the smoker's life completely and convinces him that the most precious thing on this earth is the next cigarette.

As I have already said, cutting down never works anyway because you have to exercise willpower and discipline for the rest of your life. If you had not enough willpower to stop, then you certainly have not got enough to cut down. Stopping is far easier and less painful.

I have heard of literally thousands of cases in which cutting down has failed. The handful of successes I have known have been achieved after a relatively short period of cutting down, followed by the 'cold turkey'. The smokers really stopped in spite of cutting down, not because of it. All it did was prolong the agony. A failed attempt to cut down leaves the smoker a nervous wreck, even more convinced that he is hooked for life. This is usually enough to keep him puffing away for another five years before the next attempt.

However, cutting down helps to illustrate the whole futility of smoking because it clearly illustrates that a cigarette is enjoyable only after a period of abstinence. You have to bang your head against a brick wall (i.e. suffer withdrawal pangs) to make it nice when you stop.

So the choice is:

1. Cut down for life. This will be self-imposed torture, and you will not be able to do it anyway.
2. Increasingly choke yourself for life. What is the point?
3. Be nice to yourself. Stop doing it.

The other important point that cutting down demonstrates is that there is no such thing as the odd or occasional cigarette. Smoking is a chain reaction that will last the rest of your life unless you make a positive effort to break it.

REMEMBER: CUTTING DOWN WILL DRAG YOU DOWN.

24 Just One Cigarette

'Just one cigarette' is a myth you must get out of your mind.

It is just one cigarette that gets us started in the first place.

It is just one cigarette to tide us over a difficult patch or on a special occasion that defeats most of our attempts to stop.

It is just one cigarette that, when smokers have succeeded in breaking the addiction, sends them back into the trap. Sometimes it is just to confirm that they do not need them any more, and that one cigarette does just that. It tastes horrible and convinces the smoker he will never become hooked again, but he already is.

It is the thought of that one special cigarette that often prevents smokers from stopping. The first one in the morning or the one after a meal.

Get it firmly in your mind there is no such thing as just one cigarette. It is a chain reaction that will last the rest of your life unless you break it.

It is the myth about the odd, special cigarette that keeps smokers moping about it when they stop. Get into the habit of never seeing the odd cigarette or packet – it is a fantasy. Whenever you think about smoking, see a whole filthy life-time of spending a small fortune just for the privilege of destroying yourself mentally and physically, a lifetime of slavery, a lifetime of bad breath.

It is a pity that there isn't something like a cigarette that, during good and bad times, we can use for an occasional boost or pleasure. But get it clearly into your mind: the cigarette isn't it. You are stuck with either a lifetime of misery or none at all. You wouldn't dream of taking cyanide because you liked the taste of almonds, so stop punishing yourself with the thought of the occasional cigarette or cigar.

Ask a smoker, 'If you had the opportunity to go back to the time before you became hooked, would you have become a smoker?' The answer is inevitably, 'You have got to be joking,' yet every smoker has that choice every day of his life. Why doesn't he opt for it? The answer is fear. The fear that he cannot stop or that life won't be the same without it.

Stop kidding yourself. You can do it. Anybody can. It's ridiculously easy.

In order to make it easy to stop smoking there are certain fundamentals to get clear in your mind. We have already dealt with three of them up to now:

1. There is nothing to give up. There are only marvellous positive gains to achieve.
2. Never see the odd cigarette. It doesn't exist. There is only a lifetime of filth and disease.
3. There is nothing different about you. Any smoker can find it easy to stop.

Many smokers believe that they are confirmed smokers or have addictive personalities. I promise you there is no such thing. No one needs to smoke before they become hooked on the drug. It is the drug that hooks you and not the nature of your character or personality. That is the effect of these drugs, they make you believe that you have an addictive personality. However, it is essential that you remove this belief, because if you believe that you are dependent on nicotine, you will be, even after the little nicotine monster inside your body is dead. It is essential to remove all of the brainwashing.

25 Casual Smokers, Teenagers, Non-smokers

Heavy smokers tend to envy casual smokers. We've all met these characters: 'Oh, I can go all week without a cigarette, it really doesn't bother me.' We think: 'I wish I were like that.' I know this is hard to believe, but no smoker enjoys being a smoker. Never forget:

- No smoker ever decided to become a smoker casual or otherwise, therefore:
- All smokers feel stupid, therefore:
- All smokers have to lie to themselves and other people in a vain attempt to justify their stupidity.

I used to be a golf fanatic. But I would brag about how often I played and I wanted to play more. Why do smokers brag about how little they smoke? If that's the true criterion, then surely the true accolade is not to smoke at all.

If I said to you, 'Do you know, I can go all week without carrots and it doesn't bother me in the slightest,' you would think I was some sort of nutcase. If I enjoy carrots, why would I want to go all week without them? If I didn't enjoy them, why would I make such a statement? So when a smoker makes a statement like 'I can go all week without a cigarette, it really doesn't bother me,' he's trying to convince both himself and you that he has no problem. But there would be no need to make the statement if he had no problem. What he is really saying is: 'I managed to survive a whole week without smoking.' Like every smoker, he was probably hoping that after this he could survive the rest of his life. But he could only survive a week, and can you imagine how precious that cigarette must have been, having felt deprived for a whole week?

This is why casual smokers are effectively more hooked than heavy smokers. Not only is the illusion of pleasure greater, but they have less incentive to quit because they spend less money and are less vulnerable to the health risks.

Remember, the only pleasure smokers get is to relieve withdrawal pangs and as I have already explained, even that pleasure is an illusion. Imagine the little nicotine monster inside your body as a permanent itch so imperceptible that most of the time you aren't even aware of it.

Now if you have a permanent itch, the natural tendency is to scratch it. As our bodies become more and more immune to nicotine the natural tendency is to chain-smoke.

There are three main factors that prevent smokers from chain-smoking.

1. **Money:** Most cannot afford to.
2. **Health:** In order to relieve our withdrawal pangs, we have to take a poison. Capacity to cope with that poison varies with each individual and at different times and situations in his or her life. This acts as an automatic restraint.
3. **Discipline:** This is imposed by society, or the smoker's job, or friends and relatives, or by the smoker himself as

a result of the natural tug of war that goes on in every smoker's mind.

I used to think of my chain-smoking as a weakness. I couldn't understand why my friends could limit their intake to ten or twenty a day. I knew I was a very strong-willed person. It never occurred to me that most smokers are incapable of chain-smoking, you need very strong lungs in order to do it. Some of these five-a-day smokers that heavy smokers tend to envy smoke five a day because physically their constitution cannot smoke more, or because they cannot afford to smoke more, or because their job, or society, or their own hatred of being hooked won't allow them to smoke more.

It may be of advantage at this stage to provide a few definitions.

THE NON-SMOKER. Someone who has never fallen for the trap but should not be complacent. He is a non-smoker only by the grace of God. All smokers were convinced that they would never become hooked, and some non-smokers keep trying an occasional cigarette.

THE CASUAL SMOKER. There are two basic classifications of casual smokers.

1. The smoker who has fallen for the trap but doesn't realize it. Do not envy such smokers. They are merely sampling the nectar at the mouth of the pitcher plant and in all probability will soon be heavy smokers. Remember, just as all alcoholics started off as casual drinkers, so all smokers started off as casual smokers.

2. The smoker who was previously a heavy smoker and thinks he cannot stop. These smokers are the most pathetic of all. They fall into various categories, each of which needs separate comment.

THE FIVE-A-DAY SMOKER. If he enjoys a cigarette, why does he smoke only five a day? If he can take it or leave it, why does he bother to smoke at all? Remember, the 'habit' is really banging your head against a brick wall to make it relaxing when you stop. The five-a-day smoker is relieving his withdrawal pangs for less than one hour each day. The rest of the day, although he doesn't realize it, he is banging his head against the wall and does so for most of his life. He is smoking only five a day because either he cannot afford to smoke more or he is worried about the health risk. It is easy to convince the heavy smoker that he doesn't enjoy it, but you try convincing a casual smoker. Anybody who has gone through an attempt to cut down will know it is the worst torture of all and almost guaranteed to keep you hooked for the rest of your life.

THE MORNING OR EVENING ONLY SMOKER. He punishes himself by suffering withdrawal pangs for half the day in order to relieve them the other half. Again, ask him why, if he enjoys a cigarette, he doesn't smoke the whole day or, if he doesn't enjoy a cigarette, he bothers at all.

THE SIX-MONTHS-ON, SIX-MONTHS-OFF SMOKER. (Or 'I can stop whenever I want to. I have done it thousands of times.') If he enjoys smoking, why does he stop for six months? If he does not enjoy it, why does he start again? The truth is he is still hooked. Although he gets rid of the physical addiction, he is left with the main problem – the brainwashing. He hopes each time that he will stop for good and soon falls for the trap again. Many smokers envy these stoppers and starters. They think, 'How lucky to be able to control it like that, to smoke when you want to and stop when you want to.' What they always overlook is that these stoppers and starters aren't controlling it. When they are smokers, they wish they weren't. They go through the hassle of stopping, then begin to feel deprived and fall for the trap again, then wish they hadn't. They get the worst of all worlds. When they are smokers they wish they weren't; when they are non-smokers they wish they could smoke. If you think about it, this is true all our smoking lives. When we are allowed to smoke we either take it for granted or wish we didn't. It's only when we can't have cigarettes that they appear so precious. This is the awful dilemma of smokers. They can never win because they are moping for a myth, an illusion. There is one way they can win and that is to stop smoking *and* stop moping!

THE 'I ONLY SMOKE ON SPECIAL OCCASIONS' SMOKER. Yes, we all do to start with, but isn't it amazing how the number of occasions seem rapidly to increase and before we know it we seem to be smoking on all occasions?

THE 'I HAVE STOPPED BUT I HAVE AN OCCASIONAL CIGAR/CIGARETTE' SMOKER. In a way such smokers are the most pathetic of all. Either they go through their lives believing they are being deprived or, more often, the occasional cigar becomes two. They remain on the slippery slope and it goes only one way – DOWNWARDS. Sooner or later they are back to being heavy smokers.

They have fallen again for the very trap that they fell into in the first place.

There are two other categories of casual smoker. The first is the type who smokes just the occasional cigarette or cigar at social occasions. These people are really non-smokers. They don't enjoy smoking. It's just that they feel they are missing out. They want to be part of the action. We all start off like this. Next time the cigars go round, watch how, after a while, the smokers stop relighting those cigars. Even heavy cigarette smokers can't wait to finish them. They would much rather be smoking their own brand. The more expensive and the longer the cigar, the more frustrating it is – the damn thing seems to last all night.

The second category is very rare indeed. In fact, of all the thousands who have sought my assistance, I can think of only about a dozen examples. The type can best be described by outlining a recent case.

A woman phoned me, seeking a private session. She is a solicitor, had been smoking for about twelve years and had never smoked more or less than two cigarettes a day in her smoking life. She was, incidentally, a very strong-willed lady. I explained that the success rate in group sessions was just as high as in individual sessions, and in any event I was able to give individual therapy only if the face were so famous that it would disrupt the group. She began to cry, and I was not able to resist the tears.

The session was expensive; indeed, most smokers would wonder why she wanted to stop in the first place. They would gladly pay what I charged that lady to be able to smoke only two cigarettes a day. They make the mistake of assuming that casual smokers are happier and more in control.

In control they may appear to be, but happy they are not. In this case, both the woman's parents had died from lung cancer before she became hooked. Like me, she had a great fear of smoking before she smoked the first cigarette. Like me, she eventually fell victim to the massive pressures and tried that first cigarette. Like me, she can remember the foul taste. Unlike me, who capitulated and became a chain-smoker very quickly, she resisted the slide.

All you ever enjoy in a cigarette is the ending of the craving for it, whether it be the almost imperceptible physical craving for nicotine or the mental torture caused by not being allowed to scratch the itch. Cigarettes themselves are filth and poison. This is why you only suffer the illusion of enjoying them after a period of abstinence. Just like a hunger or thirst, the longer you suffer it, the greater the pleasure when you finally relieve it. Smokers make the mistake of believing smoking is just a habit. They think, 'If I can only keep it down to a certain level or smoke only on special occasions, my brain and body will accept it. I can then keep my smoking at that level or cut down further should I wish to.' Get it clear in your mind: the 'habit' doesn't exist. Smoking is drug addiction. The natural tendency is to relieve withdrawal pangs, not to endure them. Even to hold it at the level you are already at, you would have to exercise willpower and discipline for the rest of your life because, as your body becomes immune to the drug, it wants more and more, not less and less. As the drug begins to destroy you physically and mentally, as it gradually breaks down your nervous system, your courage and confidence, so you are increasingly unable to resist reducing the interval between each cigarette. That is why, in the early days, we can take it or leave it. If we get a cold, we just stop. It also explains why someone like me, who never even suffered the illusion of enjoying them, had to go on chain-smoking even though every cigarette had become physical torture.

Don't envy that woman. When you smoke only one cigarette every twelve hours it appears to be the most precious thing on earth. For twelve years that poor woman had been at the centre of a tug of war. She had been unable to stop smoking, yet was frightened to increase the intake in case she got lung cancer like her parents. But for over twenty-three hours of every one of those days she had to fight the temptation. It took tremendous willpower to do what she did, and, as I have said, such cases are rare. But it reduced her to tears in the end. Just look at it logically: either there is a genuine crutch or pleasure in smoking or there isn't. If there is, who wants to wait an hour, or a day, or a week? Why should you be denied the crutch or pleasure in the meantime? If there is no genuine crutch or pleasure, why bother to smoke any of them?

I remember another case, that of a five-a-day man. He started the telephone conversation in a croaky voice: 'Mr Carr, I just want to stop smoking before I die.' This is how that man described his life:

'I am sixty-one years old. I have got cancer of the throat through smoking. Now I can only physically cope with five roll-ups a day. I used to sleep soundly through the night. Now I wake up every hour of the night and all I can think about is cigarettes. Even when I am sleeping, I dream about smoking.

'I cannot smoke my first cigarette until 10 o'clock. I get up at 5 o'clock and make endless cups of tea. My wife gets up about 8 o'clock and, because I am so bad-tempered, she will not have me in the house. I go down to the greenhouse and try to potter about, but my mind is obsessed with smoking. At 9 o'clock I begin to roll my first cigarette and I do so until it is perfect. It is not that I need it to be perfect, but it gives me something to do. I then wait for 10 o'clock. When it arrives my hands are shaking uncontrollably. I do not light the cigarette then. If I do, I have to wait three hours for the next one. Eventually I light the cigarette, take one puff and extinguish it immediately. By continuing this process I can make the cigarette last one hour. I smoke it down to about a quarter of an inch and then wait for the next one.'

In addition to his other troubles, this poor man had burns all over his lips caused by smoking the cigarette too low. You probably have visions of a pathetic imbecile. Not so. This man was over six feet tall and an ex-sergeant in the Marines. He was a former athlete and didn't want to become a smoker. However, in World War II society believed that cigarettes gave courage, and servicemen were issued free rations of them. This man was virtually ordered to become a smoker. He spent the rest of his life paying through the nose, subsidizing other people's taxes, and it ruined him physically and mentally. If he were an animal, our society would have put him out of his misery, yet we still allow mentally and physically healthy teenagers to become hooked.

You may think the above case is exaggerated. It is extreme but not unique. That man poured his heart out to me, but you can be sure that many of his friends and acquaintances envied him for being a five-a-day man. If you think this couldn't happen to you, STOP KIDDING YOURSELF. IT IS ALREADY HAPPENING.

In any event smokers are notorious liars, even to themselves. They have to be. Most casual smokers smoke far more cigarettes, and on far more occasions, than they will admit to. I have had many conversations with so-called five-a-day smokers during which they have smoked more than five cigarettes in my presence. Observe casual smokers at social events such as weddings and parties. They will be chain-smoking like the best of them.

You do not need to envy casual smokers. You do not need to smoke. Life is infinitely sweeter without cigarettes.

Teenagers are generally more difficult to cure, not because they find it difficult to stop but because either they do not believe they are hooked or they are at the primary stage of the disease and suffer from the delusion that they will automatically have stopped before the secondary stage.

I would like particularly to warn parents of children who loathe smoking not to have a false sense of security. All children loathe the smell and taste of tobacco until they become hooked. You did too at one time. Also do not be fooled by government scare campaigns. The trap is the same as it always was. Children know that cigarettes kill, but they also know that one cigarette will not do it. At some stage they may be influenced by a girlfriend or boyfriend, school-friend or work colleague. You may think that all they need is to try one, which will taste horrible and convince them they could never become hooked.

I find society's failure to prevent our children from becoming addicted to nicotine and other drugs to be the most disturbing of all of the many disturbing facets of drug addiction. I have given much thought to this problem and have written books designed specifically to address the problem of how to prevent your children from becoming hooked and how to help them escape if they have already done so. It is a fact that the vast majority of youngsters that become dependent on heavier drugs are introduced to the concept of chemical dependency by first falling for the nicotine trap. If you can help them avoid the nicotine trap you will greatly reduce the risk of them becoming dependent on heavier drugs. I beg you not to be complacent in this matter. It is necessary to protect youngsters at the earliest possible age and if you have a child, I strongly urge you to read those books. Even if you suspect your child might already be hooked on a drug, the books will provide excellent guidance to assist your child's escape.

26

The Secret Smoker

The secret smoker should be grouped with casual smokers, but the effects of secret smoking are so insidious that it merits a separate chapter. It can lead to the breakdown of personal relationships. In my case it nearly caused a divorce.

I was three weeks into one of my failed attempts to stop. The attempt had been triggered off by my wife's worry about my constant wheezing and coughing. I had told her I was not worried about my health. She said, 'I know you are not, but how would you feel if you had to watch someone you love systematically destroying themselves?' It was an argument that I found irresistible, hence the attempt to stop. The attempt ended after three weeks after a heated argument with an old friend. It did not register until years afterwards that my devious mind had deliberately triggered off the argument. I felt justly aggrieved at the time, but I do not believe that it was coincidence, as I had never argued with this particular friend before, nor have I since. It was clearly the little monster at work. Anyway, I had my excuse. I desperately needed a cigarette and started smoking again.

I could not bear to think of the disappointment this would cause my wife, so I did not tell her. I just smoked when alone. Then gradually I smoked in the company of friends until it got to the point where everybody knew I was smoking except my wife. I remember being quite pleased at the time. I thought, 'Well, at least it is cutting my consumption down. Eventually she accused me of continuing to smoke. I had not realized it, but she described the times I had caused an argument and stormed out of the house. At other times I had taken two hours to purchase some minor item, and on occasions when I would normally have invited her to accompany me, I had made feeble excuses to go alone.

As the antisocial split between smokers and non-smokers widens, there are literally thousands of cases where the company of friends or relatives is restricted or avoided because of this awful weed. The worst thing about secret smoking is that it supports the fallacy in the smoker's mind that he is being deprived. At the same time, it causes a major loss of self-respect; an otherwise honest person may force himself to deceive his family and friends.

It has probably happened or is still happening to you in some form.

It happened to me several times. Have you ever watched the old TV detective series *Columbo*? The theme of each episode is similar. The villain, usually a wealthy and respected businessman, has committed what he is convinced is the perfect murder, and his confidence in his crime remaining undetected receives a boost when he discovers that the rather shabby and unimpressive-looking Columbo is in charge of the case.

Columbo has this frustrating practice of closing the door after finishing his interrogation, having assured the suspect that he is in the clear, and before the satisfied look has disappeared from the murderer's face, Columbo reappears with: 'Just one small point, sir, which I'm sure you can explain . . .' The suspect stammers, and from that point on we know and he knows that Columbo will gradually wear him down.

No matter how heinous the crime, from that point on my sympathies were with the murderer. It was almost as if I were the criminal and that's exactly how those bouts of secret smoking made me feel. The hours of not being allowed to smoke, then sneaking into the garage for a crafty puff, the ten minutes of shivering in the cold, wondering where the pleasure was. The fear of being caught red-handed. Would she discover where I'd hidden the cigarettes, lighter and dog ends? The relief of returning to the house undiscovered, immediately followed by the fear that she would smell the nicotine on my breath and clothes. As I took longer and more frequent risks, the certain knowledge that sooner or later I was bound to be discovered. The final humiliation and shame when that certainty became a fact, followed by the immediate return to chain-smoking.

OH THE JOYS OF BEING A SMOKER!

27

A Social Habit?

The main reason why there are over 15 million ex-smokers in Britain since the 1960s is the social revolution that is taking place.

Yes, I know: health followed by money are the main reasons why we should want to stop, but then they always have been. We do not actually need cancer scares to tell us that cigarettes shatter our lives. These bodies of ours are the most sophisticated objects on the planet, and any smoker knows instantly, from the first puff, that cigarettes are poisonous.

The only reason why we ever get involved with smoking is the social pressure of our friends. The only valid 'plus' smoking ever had was that it was at one time considered a perfectly acceptable social habit.

Today it is generally considered, even by smokers themselves, to be thoroughly antisocial.

In the old days the strong man smoked. If you didn't smoke, you were considered a sissy, and we all worked very hard to become hooked. In every pub or club bar the majority of men would be proudly inhaling and exhaling tobacco smoke. There would be the permanent fall-out cloud, and all the ceilings that were not regularly decorated soon became yellow or brown.

Today the position is completely reversed. Today's strong man doesn't need to smoke. Today's strong man is not dependent on a drug.

With the social revolution all smokers nowadays are giving serious thought to stopping, and today's smokers are considered to be generally weak people.

The most significant trend that I have noticed since writing the first edition of this book in 1985 is the increasing emphasis on the antisocial aspect of smoking. The days when the cigarette was the proud badge of the sophisticated woman or the tough guy have gone for ever. Everyone now knows that the only reason people continue to smoke is because they have failed to stop or are too frightened to try. As smokers are bombarded by health scares, bans on smoking in public places and attacks from holier-than-thou ex-smokers, so their mannerisms are changing. I've recently seen situations that I remember as a boy but haven't seen for years, such as smokers flicking ash into their hands or pockets because they're too embarrassed to ask for an ashtray.

I was in a restaurant some years ago. It was midnight. Everyone had stopped eating. At a time when the cigarettes and cigars are normally rife, not one person was smoking. I conceitedly thought, 'Ah! I'm beginning to make an impression.' I said to the waiter, 'Is this now a non-smoking restaurant?' The reply was negative. I thought, 'That's strange. I know that a lot of people are stopping, but there must be one smoker here.' Eventually someone lit up in a corner, and the result was like a series of beacons going through the restaurant. All those other smokers had been sitting there thinking, 'Surely I can't be the only smoker here.'

Many smokers won't smoke between courses now because they feel so self-conscious leaving the restaurant to do so.

On social occasions in the open air, many not only apologize to people close to them while they are smoking but also look around to see if they'll get flak from elsewhere. As every day more and more smokers leave the sinking ship, so those left on it become terrified they'll be the last.

DON'T LET IT BE YOU!

Timing

Apart from the obvious point that as it is doing you no good, now is the right time to stop, I believe timing is important. Our society treats smoking flippantly as a slightly distasteful habit that can injure your health. It is not. It is drug addiction, a disease and the Number 1 killer in society. The worst thing that happens in most smokers' lives is getting hooked on that awful weed. If they stay hooked, horrendous things happen. Timing is important to give yourself the right to a proper cure.

First of all, identify the times or occasions when smoking appears to be important to you. If you are a businessman and smoke for the illusion of relief of stress, pick a relatively slack period; a good idea is to choose your annual holiday. If you smoke mainly during boring or relaxing periods, do the opposite. In any event take the matter seriously and make the attempt the most important thing in your life.

Look ahead for a period of about three weeks and try to anticipate any event that might lead to failure. Occasions like a wedding or Christmas need not deter you, providing you anticipate them in advance and do not feel you will be deprived. Do not attempt to cut down in the meantime, as this will only create the illusion that the cigarette is enjoyable.

In fact, it helps to force as many of the filthy things down your throat as possible. While you are smoking that last cigarette, be conscious of the bad smell and taste and think how marvellous it will be when you allow yourself to stop doing it.

WHATEVER YOU DO, DON'T FALL INTO THE TRAP OF JUST SAYING, 'NOT NOW. LATER,' AND PUTTING IT OUT OF YOUR MIND. WORK OUT YOUR TIMETABLE NOW AND LOOK FORWARD TO IT. Remember you aren't giving anything up. On the contrary: you are about to receive marvellous positive gains.

For years I've been saying I know more about the mysteries of smoking than anyone on this planet. The problem is this: although every smoker smokes purely to relieve the chemical craving for nicotine, it is not the nicotine addiction itself that hooks the smoker but the brainwashing that results from that addiction. An intelligent person will fall for a confidence trick. But only a fool will go on falling for it once he realizes that it's a confidence trick. Fortunately, most smokers aren't fools, they only think they are. Each individual smoker has his own private brainwashing. That is why there appears to be such a wide range of different types of smoker, which only serves to compound the mysteries.

With the benefit of the years of feedback that I have had since the original publication of this book, and bearing in mind that each day I learn something new about smoking, I was agreeably surprised to realize that the philosophy I propounded in the first edition was still sound. The accumulated knowledge that I have acquired over the years is how to communicate that knowledge to each individual smoker. The fact that I know every smoker can not only find it easy to stop but can actually enjoy the process is not only pointless but exceedingly frustrating unless I can make the smoker realize it.

Many people have said to me, 'You say, "Continue to smoke until you have finished the book." This tends to make the smoker take ages to read the book or just not finish it, period. Therefore you should change that instruction.' This sounds logical, but I know that if the instruction were 'Stop Immediately', some smokers wouldn't even start reading the book.

I had a smoker consult me in the early days. He said, 'I really resent having to seek your help. I know I'm strong-willed. In every other area of my life I'm in control. Why is it that all these other smokers are stopping by using their own willpower, yet I have to come to you?' He continued, 'I think I could do it on my own, if I could smoke while I was doing it.'

This may sound like a contradiction, but I know what the man meant. We think of stopping smoking as something that is very difficult to do. What do we need when we have something difficult to do? We need our little friend. So stopping smoking appears to be a double blow. Not only do we have a difficult task to perform, which is hard enough, but the crutch on which we normally rely on such occasions is no longer available.

It didn't occur to me until long after the man had left that my instruction to keep smoking is the real beauty of my method. You can continue to smoke while you go through the process of stopping. You get rid of all your doubts and fears first, and when you extinguish that final cigarette you are already a non-smoker and enjoying being one.

The only chapter that has caused me to question my

original advice seriously is this chapter on the matter of the right timing. Above I advise that if your special cigarette occasions are stress situations at the office, then pick a holiday to make an attempt to give up, and vice versa. In fact, that isn't the easiest way to do it. The easiest way is to pick what you consider to be the most *difficult* time to do it, whether it be stress, social, concentration or boredom. Once you've proved that you can cope with, and enjoy, life in the worst possible situation, every other situation becomes easy. But if I gave that as a definite instruction, would you even make the attempt to stop?

Let me use an analogy. My wife and I intend to swim together. We arrive at the pool at the same time, but we rarely swim together. The reason is that she immerses one toe, and half an hour later she's actually swimming. I cannot stand that slow torture. I know in advance that at some stage, no matter how cold the water is, eventually I'm going to have to brave it. So I've learned to do it the easy way: I dive straight in. Now, assuming that I were in a position to insist that if she didn't dive straight in, she couldn't swim at all, I know that she wouldn't swim at all. You see the problem.

From feedback I know that many smokers have used the original advice I gave on timing to delay what they think will be the evil day. My next thought was to use the technique that I used for the chapter on the advantages of smoking, something like: 'timing is very important, and in the next chapter I will advise you about the best time for you to make the attempt.' You turn the page over, and there is just a huge NOW. That is, in fact, the best advice, but would you take it?

This is the most subtle aspect of the smoking trap. When we have genuine stress in our lives, it's not the time to stop, and if we have no stress in our lives, we have no desire to stop.

Ask yourself these following questions.

When you smoked that very first cigarette, did you really decide then that you would continue to smoke the rest of your life, all day, every day, without ever being able to stop?

OF COURSE YOU DIDN'T!

Are you going to continue the rest of your life all day, every day, without ever being able to stop?

OF COURSE YOU AREN'T!

So when will you stop? Tomorrow? Next year? The year after?

Isn't this what you've been asking yourself since you first realized you were hooked? Are you hoping that one morning you will wake up and just not want to smoke any more? Stop kidding yourself. I waited thirty-three years for it to happen to me. With drug addiction you get progressively more hooked, not less. You think it will be easier tomorrow? You're still kidding yourself. If you can't do it today, what makes you think it will be easier tomorrow? Are you going to wait until you've actually contracted one of the killer diseases? That would be a bit pointless.

The real trap is the belief that now isn't the right time, that it will always be easier tomorrow.

We believe that we live stressful lives. In fact, we don't. We've taken most genuine stress out of our lives. When you leave your home you don't live in fear of being attacked by wild animals. Most of us don't have to worry where our next meal is coming from, or whether we'll have a roof over our head tonight. But just think of the life of a wild animal. Every time a rabbit comes out of its burrow, it is facing Vietnam the whole of its life. But the rabbit can handle it. It's got adrenalin and other hormones – and so have we. The truth is, the most stressful periods for any creature are early childhood and adolescence. But three billion years of natural selection have equipped us to cope with stress. I was five years old when World War II started. We were bombed, and I was separated from my parents for two years. I was billeted with people who treated me unkindly. It was an unpleasant period in my life, but I was able to cope with it. I don't believe it has left me with any permanent scars; on the contrary, I believe it has made me a stronger person. When I look back on my life there has only been one thing that I couldn't handle and that was my slavery to that damned weed.

A few years ago I thought I had all the worries in the world. I was suicidal – not in the sense that I would have jumped off a roof but in the sense that I knew that smoking would soon kill me. I argued that if this was life with my crutch, life just wouldn't be worth living without it. What I didn't realize was that when you are physically and mentally depressed everything gets you down. Now I feel like a young boy again. Only one thing made the change in my life: I'm now out of the smoking pit.

I know it's a cliché to say, 'If you haven't got your health, you've got nothing,' but it's absolutely true. I used to think that physical-fitness fanatics like Gary Player were a pain. I used to claim there's more to life than feeling fit; there's booze and tobacco. That's nonsense. When you feel physically and mentally strong you can enjoy the highs and handle the lows. We confuse responsibility with stress. Responsibility becomes stressful only when you don't feel strong enough to handle it. The Richard Burtons of this world are physically and mentally strong. What destroys them is not the stresses of life, or their jobs, or old age but the so-called crutches they turn to, which are just illusions. Sadly, in his case and for millions like him, the crutches kill.

Look at it this way. You've already decided that you are not going to stay in the trap the rest of your life. Therefore at some time in your life, whether you find it easy or difficult, you will have to go through the process of getting free. Smoking is not a habit or a pleasure. It is drug addiction and a disease. We've already established that, far from being easier to stop tomorrow, it will get progressively harder. With a disease that's going to get progressively worse, the time to get rid of it is NOW – or as near to now as you can manage. Just think how quickly each week of our lives comes and goes. That's all it takes. Just think how nice it will be to enjoy the rest of your life without that ever-increasing black shadow hanging over you. And if you follow all my instructions, you won't even have to wait five days. You won't only find it easy after extinguishing the final cigarette: YOU'LL ENJOY IT!

29 Will I Miss the Cigarette?

No! Once that little nicotine monster is dead and your body stops craving nicotine, any remaining brainwashing will vanish and you will find that you will be both physically and mentally better equipped not only to cope with the stresses and strains of life but to enjoy the good times to the full.

There is only one danger and that is the influence of people who are still smoking. 'The other man's grass is always greener' is commonplace in many aspects of our lives and is easily understandable. Why is it in the case of smoking, where the disadvantages are so enormous as compared with even the illusory 'advantages', that ex-smokers tend to envy the smoker?

With all the brainwashing of our childhood it is quite understandable that we fall into the trap. Why is it that, once we realize what a mug's game it is and many of us manage to kick it, we walk straight back into the same trap? It is the influence of smokers.

It usually happens on social occasions, particularly after a meal. The smoker lights up and the ex-smoker has a pang. This is indeed a curious anomaly, particularly if you consider this piece of market research: not only is every non-smoker in the world happy to be a non-smoker but every smoker in the world, even with his warped, addicted, brainwashed mind suffering the delusion that he enjoys it or it relaxes him, wishes he had never become hooked in the first place. So why do some ex-smokers envy the smoker on these occasions? There are two reasons:

1. 'Just one cigarette.' Remember: it doesn't exist. Stop seeing that isolated occasion and start looking at it from the point of view of the smoker. You may be envying him, but he doesn't approve of himself: He envies you. Start observing other smokers. They can be the most powerful boost of all to help you off it. Notice how quickly the cigarette burns, how quickly the smoker has to light up another. Notice particularly that not only is he not aware that he is smoking the cigarette but even the lighting up appears to be automatic. Remember, he is not enjoying it; it's just that he cannot enjoy himself without it. Particularly remember that when he leaves your company he is going to have to go on smoking. The next morning, when he wakes up with a chest like a cesspit, he is going to have to carry on choking himself; the next Budget Day; the next time he has a pain in the chest; the next National No-Smoking Day; the next time he inadvertently sees the government health warning; the next time there is a cancer scare; the next time he is in church, on a train, visiting a hospital, library, dentist, doctor, supermarket, etc; the next time he is in the company of a non-smoker; he has to continue this lifetime chain of paying through the nose just for the privilege of destroying himself physically and mentally. He is facing a lifetime of filth, bad breath and stained teeth; a lifetime of slavery; a lifetime of destroying himself; a lifetime of black shadows at the back of his mind. And all

of this is to achieve what purpose? The illusion of trying to get back to the state he was in before he became hooked in the first place.

2. The second reason why some ex-smokers have pangs on these occasions is because the smoker is doing something, i.e. smoking a cigarette, and the non-smoker is not, so he tends to feel deprived. Get it clear in your mind before you start: it is not the non-smoker who is being deprived. It is the poor smoker who is being deprived of

HEALTH
ENERGY
MONEY
CONFIDENCE
PEACE OF MIND
COURAGE
TRANQUILLITY
FREEDOM
SELF-RESPECT

Stop envying smokers and start seeing them as the miserable, pathetic creatures they really are. I know: I was the world's worst. That is why you are reading this book, and the ones who cannot face up to it, who have to go on kidding themselves, are the most pathetic of all.

You wouldn't envy a heroin addict. Heroin kills a few hundred people a year in the UK. Nicotine kills over 110,000 a year and 4 million a year worldwide. It's already killed more people on this planet than all the wars of history combined. Like all drug addiction, it won't get better. Each year it will get worse and worse. If you don't enjoy being a smoker today, you'll enjoy it even less tomorrow. Don't envy other smokers. Pity them. Believe me, THEY DESERVE YOUR PITY.

30

Will I Put on Weight?

This is another myth about smoking, spread mainly by smokers who, when attempting to stop on the Willpower Method, substitute sweets, etc, to try to relieve withdrawal pangs. The withdrawal pangs of nicotine are very similar to hunger pangs, and the two are easily confused. However, whereas the pangs of hunger can be satisfied by food, the withdrawal pangs of nicotine are never completely satisfied.

As with any drug, after a while the body becomes immune and the drug ceases to relieve the withdrawal pangs completely. As soon as we extinguish a cigarette, the nicotine rapidly leaves our body, so that the nicotine addict has a permanent hunger. The natural inclination is eventually to chain-smoke. However, most smokers are prevented from doing this for one, or both, of two reasons.

1. Money – they cannot afford to increase their intake.
2. Health – in order to relieve the withdrawal pangs we have to intake a poison, which acts as an automatic check on the number of cigarettes we can smoke.

The smoker is therefore left with a permanent hunger that he can never satisfy. This is why many smokers turn to overeating, heavy drinking or even harder drugs in order to satisfy the void. (MOST ALCOHOLICS ARE HEAVY SMOKERS. I WONDER IF IT IS REALLY A SMOKING PROBLEM?)

For the smoker the normal tendency is to start by substituting nicotine for food. During my own nightmare years I got to the stage where I cut out breakfast and lunch completely. I would chain-smoke during the day. In the later years I would actually look forward to the evenings only because then I could stop smoking. However, I would be picking at food all evening. I thought it was hunger, but it was really the withdrawal pangs from nicotine. In other words, during the days I would substitute nicotine for food and during the evenings I would substitute food for nicotine.

In those days I was two stone heavier than I am now and there was nothing I could do about it.

Once that little monster leaves your body, the awful feeling of insecurity ends. Your confidence returns, together with a marvellous feeling of self-respect. You obtain the assurance to take control of your life, not only in your eating habits but also in all other ways. This is one of the many great advantages of being free from the weed.

As I have said, the weight myth is due to using substitutes during the withdrawal period. In fact, they do not make it easier to stop. They make it harder. This is explained in greater detail in chapter 37, which deals with substitutes.

Provided you follow all the instructions, weight gain should not be a problem to you. However, if you already have weight problems, or find that your weight does become a problem, I would recommend that you read 'Allen Carr's

EASYWEIGH to Lose Weight' (Penguin) which is based on exactly the same principles as 'EASYWAY' and makes weight control a pleasure.

31

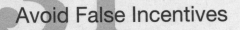

Avoid False Incentives

Many smokers, while trying to stop on the Willpower Method, try to increase the motivation to stop by building up false incentives.

There are many examples of this. A typical one is 'My family and I can have a marvellous holiday on the money I will save.' This appears to be a logical and sensible approach, but in fact it is false because any self-respecting smoker would rather smoke fifty-two weeks in the year and not have a holiday. In any case there is a doubt in the smoker's mind because not only will he have to abstain for fifty weeks but will he even enjoy that holiday without a cigarette? All this does is to increase the sacrifice that the smoker feels he is making, which makes the cigarette even more precious in his mind. Instead concentrate on the other side: 'What am I getting out of it? Why do I need to smoke?' Another example: 'I'll be able to afford a better car.' That's true, and the incentive may make you abstain until you get that car, but once the novelty has gone you will feel deprived, and sooner or later you will fall for the trap again.

Another typical example is office or family pacts. These have the advantage of eliminating temptation for certain periods of the day. However, they generally fail for the following reasons:

1. The incentive is false. Why should you want to stop smoking just because other people are doing so? All this does is to create an additional pressure, which increases the feeling of sacrifice. It is fine if all smokers genuinely want to stop at one particular time. However, you cannot force smokers to stop, and although all smokers secretly want to, until they are ready to do so a pact just creates additional pressure, which increases their desire to smoke. This turns them into secret smokers, which further increases the feeling of dependency.

2. The 'Rotten Apple' principle, or dependency on each other. Under the Willpower Method of stopping, the smoker is undergoing a period of penance during which he waits for the urge to smoke to go. If he gives in, there is a sense of failure. Under the Willpower Method one of the participants is bound to give in sooner or later. The other participants now have the excuse they have been waiting for. It's not their fault. They would have held out. It is just that Fred has let them down. The truth is that most of them have already been cheating.

3. 'Sharing the credit' is the reverse of the 'Rotten apple' theory. Here the loss of face due to failure is not so bad when shared. There is a marvellous sense of achievement in stopping smoking. When you are doing it alone the acclaim you receive from your friends, relatives and colleagues can be a tremendous boost to help you over the first few days. When everybody is doing it at the same time the credit has to be shared and the boost is consequently reduced.

Another classic example of false incentives is the bribe (e.g. the parent offering the teenager a sum of money to abstain or the bet, 'I will give you £100 if I fail'). There was once an example in a TV programme. A policeman trying to give up smoking put a £20 note in his cigarette packet. He had a pact with himself. He could smoke again, but he had to set light first to the £20 note. This stopped him for a few days, but eventually he burnt the note.

Stop kidding yourself. If the £75,000 that the average smoker spends in his life won't stop him, or the one-in-two risk of horrendous diseases, or the lifetime of bad breath, mental and physical torture and slavery or being despised by most of the population and despising yourself, a few phony incentives will not make the slightest bit of difference. They will only make the sacrifice appear worse. Keep looking at the other side of the tug of war.

What is smoking doing for me? ABSOLUTELY NOTHING.

Why do I need to do it? YOU DON'T! YOU ARE ONLY PUNISHING YOURSELF.

32

The Easy Way to Stop

This chapter contains instructions about the easy way to stop smoking. Providing you follow the instructions, you will find that stopping ranges from relatively easy to enjoyable! But remember the definition of a brunette: 'a girl who didn't read the instructions on the bottle'.

It is ridiculously easy to stop smoking. All you have to do is two things.

1. Make the decision that you are never going to smoke again.
2. Don't mope about it. Rejoice.

You are probably asking, 'Why the need for the rest of the book? Why couldn't you have said that in the first place?' The answer is that you would at some time have moped about it, and consequently, sooner or later, you would have changed your decision. You have probably already done it many times before.

As I have already said, the whole business of smoking is a subtle, sinister trap. The main problem of stopping isn't the chemical addiction but the brainwashing, and it was necessary first to explode the myths and delusions. Understand your enemy. Know his tactics, and you will easily defeat him.

I've spent much of my life trying to stop smoking and I've suffered weeks of black depression. When I finally stopped I went from a hundred a day to zero without one bad moment. It was enjoyable even during the withdrawal period, and I have never had the slightest pang since. On the contrary, it is the most wonderful thing that has happened in my life.

I couldn't understand why it had been so easy and it took me a long time to find out the reason. It was this. I knew for certain that I was never going to smoke again. During previous attempts, no matter how determined I was, I was basically *trying* to stop smoking, hoping that if I could survive long enough without a cigarette, the urge would eventually go. Of course it didn't go because I was waiting for something to happen, and the more I moped about it, the more I wanted a cigarette, so the craving never went.

My final attempt was different. Like all smokers nowadays, I had been giving the problem serious thought. Up to then, whenever I failed, I had consoled myself with the thought that it would be easier next time. It had never occurred to me that I would have to go on smoking for the rest of my life. This latter thought filled me with horror and started me thinking very deeply about the subject.

Instead of lighting up cigarettes subconsciously, I began to analyse my feelings as I was smoking them. This confirmed what I already knew. I wasn't enjoying them, and they were filthy and disgusting.

I started looking at non-smokers. Until then I had always regarded non-smokers as wishy-washy, unsociable, finicky people. However, when I examined them they appeared, if anything, stronger and more relaxed. They appeared to be able to cope with the stresses and strains of life, and they seemed to enjoy social functions more than the smokers. They certainly had more sparkle and zest than smokers.

I started talking to ex-smokers. Up to this point I had regarded ex-smokers as people who had been forced to give up smoking for health and money reasons and who were always secretly longing for a cigarette. A few did say, 'You get the odd pangs, but they are so few and far between they aren't worth bothering about.' But most said, 'Miss it? You must be joking. I have never felt better in my life.'

Talking to ex-smokers exploded another myth that I had always had in my mind. I had thought that there was an inherent weakness in me, and it suddenly dawned on me that all smokers go through this private nightmare. Basically I said to myself, 'Millions of people are stopping now and leading perfectly happy lives. I didn't need to do it before I started, and I can remember having to work hard to get used to the filthy things. So why do I need to do it now?' In any event I didn't enjoy smoking. I hated the whole filthy ritual and I didn't want to spend the rest of my life being the slave of this disgusting weed.

I then said to myself: 'Allen, WHETHER YOU LIKE IT OR NOT, YOU HAVE SMOKED YOUR LAST CIGARETTE.'

I knew, right from that point, that I would never smoke again. I wasn't expecting it to be easy; in fact, just the reverse. I fully believed that I was in for months of black depression and that I would spend the rest of my life having the occasional pang. Instead it has been absolute bliss right from the start.

It took me a long time to work out why it had been so easy and why this time I hadn't suffered those terrifying withdrawal pangs. The reason is that they do not exist. It is the doubt and uncertainty that cause the pangs. The beautiful truth is: IT IS EASY TO STOP SMOKING. It is only the indecision and moping about it that make it difficult. Even while they are addicted to nicotine, smokers can go for relatively long periods at certain times in their lives without bothering about it. It is only when you want a cigarette but can't have one that you suffer.

Therefore the key to making it easy is to make stopping certain and final. Not to *hope* but to *know* you have kicked it, having made the decision. Never to doubt or question it. In fact, just the reverse – always to rejoice about it.

If you can be certain from the start, it will be easy. But how can you be certain from the start unless you know it is going to be easy? This is why the rest of the book is necessary. There are certain essential points and it is necessary to get them clear in our mind before you start.

1. Realize that you can achieve it. There is nothing different about you, and the only person who can make you smoke that next cigarette is you.
2. There is absolutely nothing to give up. On the contrary, there are enormous positive gains to be made. I do not only mean you will be healthier and richer. I mean you will enjoy the good times more and be less miserable during the bad times.
3. Get it clear in your mind that there is no such thing as one cigarette. Smoking is a drug addiction and a chain reaction. By moaning about the odd cigarette you will only be punishing yourself needlessly.
4. See the whole business of smoking not as a sociable habit that might injure you, but as drug addiction. Face up to the fact that, whether you like it or not, YOU HAVE

GOT THE DISEASE. It will not go away because you bury your head in the sand. Remember: like all crippling diseases, it not only lasts for life but gets worse and worse. The easiest time to cure it is *now*.

5. Separate the disease (i.e. the chemical addiction) from the frame of mind of being a smoker or a non-smoker. All smokers, if given the opportunity to go back to the time before they became hooked, would jump at that opportunity. You have that opportunity today! Don't even think about it as 'giving up' smoking. When you have made the final decision that you have smoked your last cigarette you will already be a non-smoker. A smoker is one of those poor wretches who have to go through life destroying themselves with cigarettes. A non-smoker is someone who doesn't. Once you have made that final decision, you have already achieved your object. Rejoice in the fact. Do not sit moping waiting for the chemical addiction to go. Get out and enjoy life immediately. Life is marvellous even when you are addicted to nicotine, and each day it will get better when you aren't.

The key to making it easy to quit smoking is to be certain that you will succeed in abstaining completely during the withdrawal period (maximum three weeks). If you are in the correct frame of mind, you will find it ridiculously easy.

By this stage, if you have opened your mind as I requested at the beginning, you will already have decided you are going to stop. You should now have a feeling of excitement, like a dog straining at the lead, unable to wait to get the poison out of your system.

If you have a feeling of doom and gloom, it will be for one of the following reasons.

1. Something has not gelled in your mind. Re-read the above five points, and ask yourself if you believe them to be true. If you doubt any point, re-read the appropriate sections in the book.
2. You fear failure itself. Do not worry. Just read on. You will succeed. The whole business of smoking is like a confidence trick on a gigantic scale. Intelligent people fall for confidence tricks, but it is only a fool who, having once found out about the trick, goes on kidding himself.
3. You agree with everything, but you are still miserable. Don't be! Open your eyes. Something marvellous is happening. You are about to escape from the prison.

It is essential to start with the correct frame of mind: isn't it marvellous that I am a non-smoker!

All we have to do now is to keep you in that frame of mind during the withdrawal period, and the next few chapters deal with specific points to enable you to stay in that frame of mind during that time. After the withdrawal period you won't have to think that way. You will think that way automatically, and the only mystery in your life will be 'It is so obvious, why couldn't I see it before?' However, two important warnings:

1. Delay your plan to extinguish your last cigarette until you have finished the book.
2. I have mentioned several times a withdrawal period of up to three weeks. This can cause misunderstanding. First, you may subconsciously feel that you have to suffer for three weeks. You don't. Secondly, avoid the trap of thinking, 'Somehow I have just got to abstain for three weeks and then I will be free.' Nothing will actually happen after

three weeks. You won't suddenly feel like a non-smoker. Non-smokers do not feel any different from smokers. If you are moping about stopping during the three weeks, in all probability you will still be moping about it after the three weeks. What I am saying is, if you can start right now by saying, 'I am never going to smoke again. Isn't it marvellous?' after three weeks all temptation will go. Whereas if you say, 'If only I can survive three weeks without a cigarette,' you will be dying for a cigarette after the three weeks are up.

33

The Withdrawal Period

For up to three weeks after your last cigarette you may be subjected to withdrawal pangs. These consist of two quite separate factors.

1. The withdrawal pangs of nicotine, that empty, insecure feeling, like a hunger, which smokers identify as a craving or a need for something to do with their hands.
2. The psychological trigger of certain events such as a telephone conversation.

It is the failure to understand and to differentiate between these two factors that makes it so difficult for smokers to achieve success on the Willpower Method, and it's also the reason why many smokers who do achieve it fall into the trap again.

Although the withdrawal pangs of nicotine cause no physical pain, do not underestimate their power. We talk of 'hunger pains' if we go without food for a day; there may be 'tummy rumblings', but there is no physical pain. Even so, hunger is a powerful force, and we are likely to become very irritable when deprived of food. It is similar when our body is craving nicotine. The difference is that our body needs food but it doesn't need poison and with the right frame of mind the withdrawal pangs are easily overcome and disappear very quickly.

If smokers can abstain for a few days on the Willpower Method, the craving for nicotine soon disappears. It is the second factor that causes the difficulty. The smoker has got into the habit of relieving his withdrawal pangs at certain times or occasions, which causes an association of ideas (e.g. 'I cannot enjoy a drink without a cigarette'). It may be easier to understand the effect with the help of an example.

You have a car for a few years, and let's say the indicator lever is on the left of the steering column. On your next car it is on the right (the law of Sod). You know it is on the right, but for a couple of weeks you put the windscreen wipers on whenever you want to indicate.

Stopping smoking is similar. During the early days of the withdrawal period the trigger mechanism will operate at certain times. You will think, 'I want a cigarette.' It is essential to counter the brainwashing right from square one, then these automatic triggers will quickly disappear. Under the Willpower Method, because the smoker believes he is making a sacrifice, is moping about it and is waiting for the urge to smoke to go, far from removing these trigger mechanisms he is actually increasing them.

A common trigger is a meal, particularly one with friends. The ex-smoker is already miserable because he is being deprived of his cigarette. His friends light up and he feels even more deprived. Now he is not enjoying the meal or what should be a pleasant social occasion. Because of his association of the cigarette with the meal and the social occasion he is now suffering a triple blow, and the brainwashing is actually being increased. If he is resolute and can hold out long enough, he eventually accepts his lot and gets on with his life. However, part of the brainwashing remains, and I think the second most pathetic thing about smoking is the smoker who has given up for health or money reasons, yet even after several years still craves a cigarette on certain occasions. He is pining for an illusion that exists only in his mind and is needlessly torturing himself.

Even under my method responding to triggers is the most common failing. The ex-smoker tends to regard the cigarette as a sort of placebo or sugar pill. He thinks: 'I know the cigarette does nothing for me, but if I think it does, on certain occasions it will be a help to me.'

A sugar pill, although giving no actual physical help, can be a powerful psychological aid to relieve genuine symptoms and is therefore a benefit. The cigarette, however, is not a sugar pill. It creates the symptoms that it relieves and after a while ceases even to relieve these symptoms completely; the 'pill' is causing the disease, and quite apart from that it also happens to be the Number 1 killer poison in society.

You may find it easier to understand the effect when related to non-smokers or a smoker who has quit for several years. Take the case of a wife who loses her husband. It is quite common at such times for a smoker, with the best intentions, to say, 'Have a cigarette. It will help calm you down.'

If the cigarette is accepted, it will not have a calming effect because the woman is not addicted to nicotine and there are no withdrawal pangs to relieve. At best all it will do is to give her a momentary psychological boost. As soon as the cigarette is extinguished, the original tragedy is still there. In fact, it will be increased because the woman is now suffering withdrawal pangs, and her choice is now either to endure them or to relieve them by smoking another cigarette and starting the chain of misery. All the cigarette will have done is to give a momentary psychological boost. The same effect could have been achieved by offering a word of comfort or a cup of tea. Many non-smokers and ex-smokers have become addicted to the weed as a result of such occasions.

It is essential to counter the brainwashing right from the start. Get it quite clear in your head: you don't need the cigarette, and you are only torturing yourself by continuing to regard it as some sort of prop or boost. There is no need to be miserable. Cigarettes do not make meals or social occasions; they ruin them. Remember too that the smokers at that meal are not smoking because they are enjoying the cigarette. They are smoking because they have got to. They are drug addicts. They cannot enjoy the meal or life without it.

Abandon the idea that smoking is pleasurable in itself. Many smokers think, 'If only there were a clean cigarette.' There *are* clean cigarettes. Any smoker who tries a herbal cigarette soon finds out they are a waste of time. Get it clear in your mind that the only reason you have been smoking is to get the nicotine. Once you have got rid of the craving for nicotine you will have no more need to stick a cigarette in your mouth than in your ear.

Whether the pang is due to actual withdrawal symptoms (the empty feeling) or a trigger mechanism, accept it. The physical pain is non-existent and with the right frame of mind cigarettes become no problem. Do not worry about withdrawal. The feeling itself isn't bad. It is the association with wanting a cigarette and then feeling denied that is the problem.

Instead of moping about it, say to yourself, 'I know what it is. It's the withdrawal pang from nicotine. That's what smokers suffer all their lives and that's what keeps them smoking. Non-smokers do not suffer these pangs. It is another of the many evils of this drug. Isn't it marvellous I am purging this evil from my body!'

In other words, for the next three weeks you will have a slight trauma inside your body, but during those weeks, and for the rest of your life, something marvellous will be happening. You will be ridding yourself of an awful disease. That bonus will more than outweigh the slight trauma, and you will actually enjoy the withdrawal pangs. They will become moments of pleasure.

Think of the whole business of stopping as an exciting game. Think of the nicotine monster as a sort of tapeworm inside your stomach. You have got to starve him for three weeks, and he is going to try and trick you into lighting a cigarette to keep him alive.

At times he will try to make you miserable. At times you will be off guard. Someone may offer you a cigarette and you may forget that you have stopped. There is a slight feeling of deprivation when you remember. Be prepared for these traps in advance. Whatever the temptation, get it into your mind that it is only there because of the monster inside your body, and every time you resist the temptation you have dealt another mortal blow in the battle.

Whatever you do, don't try to forget about smoking. This is one of the things that causes smokers using the Willpower Method hours of depression. They try to get through each day hoping that eventually they'll just forget about it.

It is like not being able to sleep. The more you worry about it, the harder it becomes.

In any event you won't be able to forget about it. For the first few days the 'little monster' will keep reminding you, and you won't be able to avoid it; while there are still smokers and extensive cigarette promotions about, you will have constant reminders.

The point is, you have no need to forget. Nothing bad is happening. Something marvellous is taking place. Even if you are thinking about it a thousand times a day, SAVOUR EACH MOMENT. REMIND YOURSELF HOW MARVELLOUS IT IS TO BE FREE AGAIN. REMIND YOURSELF OF THE SHEER JOY OF NOT HAVING TO CHOKE YOURSELF ANY MORE.

As I have said, you will find that the pangs become moments of pleasure, and you will be surprised how quickly you will then forget about smoking.

Whatever you do – DO NOT DOUBT YOUR DECISION. Once you start to doubt, you will start to mope, and it will get worse. Instead use the moment as a boost. If the cause is depression, remind yourself that's what cigarettes were doing to you. If you are offered one by a friend, take pride in saying, 'I'm happy to say I do not need them any more.' That will hurt him, but when he sees that it isn't bothering you he will be halfway to joining you.

Remember that you had very powerful reasons for stopping in the first place. Remind yourself of the £xx,ooo that one cigarette will cost you, and ask yourself whether you really want to risk those fearful diseases. Above all, remember that the feeling is only temporary and each moment is a moment nearer to your goal.

Some smokers fear that they will have to spend the rest of their lives reversing the 'automatic triggers'. In other words, they believe that they will have to go through life kidding themselves that they don't really need a cigarette by the use of psychology. This is not so. Remember that the optimist sees the bottle as half full and the pessimist sees it as half empty. In the case of smoking, the bottle is empty and the smoker sees it as full. It is the smoker who has been brainwashed. Once you start telling yourself that you don't need to smoke, in a very short time you won't even need to say it because the beautiful truth is . . . you do not need to smoke. It's the last thing you need to do; make sure it's not the last thing you do.

34
Just One Puff

This is the undoing of many smokers who try to stop on the Willpower Method. They will go through three or four days and then have the odd cigarette or a puff or two to tide them over. They do not realize the devastating effect this has on their morale.

For most smokers that first puff doesn't taste good, and this gives their conscious minds a boost. They think, 'Good. That wasn't enjoyable. I am losing the urge to smoke.' In fact, the reverse is the case. Get it clear in your mind – CIGARETTES NEVER WERE ENJOYABLE. Enjoyment wasn't the reason why you smoked. If smokers smoked for enjoyment, they'd never smoke more than one cigarette.

The only reason why you smoked was to feed that little monster. Just think: you had starved him for four days. How precious that one cigarette or just the puff must have been to him. You are not aware of it in your conscious mind, but the fix your body received will be communicated to your subconscious mind and all your sound preparation will be undermined. There will be a little voice at the back of your mind saying, 'In spite of all the logic, they are precious. I want another one.'

That little puff has two damaging effects.

1. It keeps the little monster alive in your body.
2. What's worse, it keeps the big monster alive in your mind. If you had the last puff, it will be easier to have the next one.

Remember: just one cigarette is how people get into smoking in the first place.

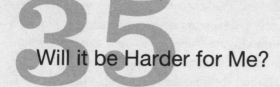

Will it be Harder for Me?

The combinations of factors that will determine how easily each individual smoker will quit are infinite. To start with, each of us has his own character, type of work, personal circumstances, timing, etc.

Certain professions may make it harder than others, but providing the brainwashing is removed it doesn't have to be so. A few individual examples will help.

It tends to be particularly difficult for members of the medical profession. We think it should be easier for doctors because they are more aware of the effects of ill-health and are seeing daily evidence of it. Although this supplies more forceful reasons for stopping, it doesn't make it any easier to do. The reasons are these:

1. The constant awareness of the health risks creates fear, which is one of the conditions under which we need to relieve our withdrawal pangs.
2. A doctor's work is exceedingly stressful, and he is usually not able to relieve the additional stress of withdrawal pangs while he is working.
3. He has the additional stress of guilt. He feels that he should be setting an example for the rest of the population.

This puts more pressure on him and increases the feeling of deprivation.

During his hard-earned breaks, when the normal stress is momentarily relieved, that cigarette becomes very precious when he eventually relieves his withdrawal pangs. This is a form of casual smoking and applies to any situation where the smoker is forced to abstain for lengthy periods. Under the Willpower Method the smoker is miserable because he is being deprived. He is not enjoying the break or the cup of tea or coffee that goes with it. His sense of loss is therefore greatly increased and, because of the association of ideas, the cigarette gets credit for the total situation. However, if you can first remove the brainwashing and stop moping about the cigarette, the break and the cup of tea can still be enjoyed even while the body is craving nicotine.

Another difficult situation is boredom, particularly when it is combined with periods of stress. Typical examples are drivers or housewives with young children. The work is stressful, yet much of the work is monotonous. During an attempt to stop on the Willpower Method the housewife has long periods in which to mope about her 'loss', which increases the feeling of depression.

Again this can be easily overcome if your frame of mind is correct. Do not worry that you are continually reminded that you have stopped smoking. Use such moments to rejoice in the fact that you are ridding yourself of the evil monster. If you have a positive frame of mind, these pangs can become moments of pleasure.

Remember, any smoker, regardless of age, sex, intelligence or profession, can find it easy and enjoyable to stop provided YOU FOLLOW ALL THE INSTRUCTIONS.

36
The Main Reasons for Failure

There are two main reasons for failure. The first is the influence of other smokers. At a weak moment or during a social occasion somebody will light up. I have already dealt with this topic at length. Use that moment to remind yourself that there is no such thing as just one cigarette. Rejoice in the fact that you have broken the chain. Remember that the smoker envies you, and feel sorry for him. Believe me, he needs your pity.

The other main reason for failure is having a bad day. Get it clear in your mind before you start that, whether you are a smoker or a non-smoker, there are good days and bad days. Life is a matter of relativity, and you cannot have ups without having downs.

The problem with the Willpower Method of stopping is that as soon as the smoker has a bad day he starts moping for a cigarette, and all he does is make a bad day worse. The non-smoker is better equipped, not only physically but also mentally, to cope with the stresses and strains of life.

If you have a bad day during the withdrawal period, just take it on the chin. Remind yourself that you had bad days when you smoked (otherwise you wouldn't have decided to stop). Instead of moping about it, say to yourself something like, 'OK, today's not so good, but smoking is not going to cure it. Tomorrow will be better, and at least I have got a marvellous bonus at the moment. I'm free from the awful slavery of smoking.'

When you are a smoker you have to block your mind to the bad side of smoking. Smokers never have smokers' coughs, just permanent colds. When your car breaks down in the middle of nowhere you light a cigarette, but are you happy and cheerful? Of course you aren't. Once you stop smoking the tendency is to blame everything that goes wrong in your life on the fact that you have stopped. Now if your car breaks down, you think, 'At times like this I would have lit a cigarette.' That's true, but what you forget is that the cigarette didn't solve the problem, and you are simply punishing yourself by moping for an illusory crutch. You are creating an impossible situation. You are miserable because you can't have the cigarette, and you'll be even more miserable if you do. You know that you have made the correct decision by stopping smoking, so don't punish yourself by ever doubting the decision.

Remember: a positive mental approach is essential – always.

37
Substitutes

Substitutes include chewing gum, sweets, peppermints, herbal cigarettes, potions and pills. DO NOT USE ANY OF THEM. They make it harder, not easier. If you do get a pang and use a substitute, it will prolong the pang and make it harder. What you are really saying is, 'I need to smoke or fill the void.' It will be like giving in to a hijacker or the tantrums of a child. It will just keep the pangs coming and prolong the torture. In any event the substitutes will not relieve the pangs. Your craving is for nicotine, not food. All it will do is keep you thinking about smoking. Remember these points:

1. There is no substitute for nicotine.
2. You do not need nicotine. It is not food; it is poison. When the pangs come remind yourself that it is smokers who suffer withdrawal pangs, not non-smokers. See them as another evil of the drug. See them as the death of a monster.
3. Remember: cigarettes create the void; they do not fill it. The quicker you teach your brain that you do not need to smoke, or do anything else in its place, the sooner you will be free.

In particular avoid any product that contains nicotine, whether it be gum, patches, nasal spray, inhalator or whatever the latest nicotine gimmick might be. It is true that a small proportion of smokers who attempt to quit using nicotine substitutes do succeed and attribute their success to such use. However they quit in spite of their use and not because of it. It is unfortunate that many doctors still recommend nicotine replacement therapy (NRT).

This is not surprising because, if you don't fully understand the nicotine trap, NRT sounds very logical. It is based on the belief that when you attempt to quit smoking, you have two powerful enemies to defeat:

1. To break the habit.
2. To survive the terrible physical nicotine withdrawal pains.

If you have two powerful enemies to defeat it is sensible not to fight them simultaneously but one at a time. So the NRT theory is that you first stop smoking but continue to take a nicotine replacement. Then, once you have broken the habit, you gradually reduce the supply of nicotine, thus tackling each enemy separately.

It sounds logical, but it is based on the wrong facts. Smoking is not habit but nicotine addiction and the actual physical pain from nicotine withdrawal is almost imperceptible. What you are trying to achieve when you quit smoking is to kill both the little nicotine monster in your body and the big monster inside your brain as quickly as possible. All NRT does is to prolong the life of the little monster which in turn will prolong the life of the big monster.

Remember EASYWAY makes it easy to quit immediately. You can kill the big monster (brainwashing) before you extinguish your final cigarette. The little monster will soon be dead and even whilst it is dying, will be no more of a problem than it was when you were a smoker.

Just think, how can you possibly cure an addict of addiction to a drug by recommending the same drug? One eminent and highly respected doctor has actually stated on national television that some smokers are so dependent on nicotine that if they did quit they would have to take a nicotine substitute for life. How can a doctor get so confused as to believe that the human body is not just dependent upon food, water and oxygen, but on a powerful poison?

We often have smokers attend our clinics who have quit smoking but are hooked on nicotine gum. Others are hooked on the gum and are still smoking. Do not be fooled by the fact that the gum tastes awful – so did the first cigarette.

All substitutes have exactly the same effect as nicotine chewing gum. I'm now talking about this business of 'I can't have a cigarette, so I'll have ordinary chewing gum, or sweets, or peppermints to help fill the void.' Although the empty feeling of wanting a cigarette is indistinguishable from hunger for food, one will not satisfy the other. In fact, if anything is designed to make you want a cigarette, it's stuffing yourself with chewing gum or peppermints.

But the chief evil of substitutes is that they prolong the real problem, which is the brainwashing. Do you need a substitute for flu when it's over? Of course you don't. By saying, 'I need a substitute for smoking,' what you are really saying is 'I am making a sacrifice.' The depression associated with the Willpower Method is caused by the fact that the smoker believes he is making a sacrifice. All you will be doing is to substitute one problem for another. There is no pleasure in stuffing yourself with sweets. You will just get fat and miserable, and in no time at all you'll be back on the weed.

Casual smokers find it difficult to dismiss the belief that they are being deprived of their little reward: the cigarette during their break from work; teachers having a quick one between lessons; or the quickie by doctors between patients. Some say: 'I wouldn't even take the break if I didn't smoke.' That proves the point, often the break is taken, not because the smoker needs it or even wants it, but because the smoker desperately needs to scratch the itch. Remember, those cigarettes never were genuine rewards. They were equivalent to wearing tight shoes to get the pleasure of taking them off. So if you feel that you must have a little reward, let that be your substitute; while you are working, wear a pair of shoes a size too small for you, don't allow yourself to remove them until you have your break, then experience that wonderful moment of relaxation and satisfaction when you do remove them. Perhaps you feel that would be rather stupid. You are absolutely right. It's hard to visualize while you are still in the trap, but that is what smokers do. It's also hard to visualize that soon you won't need that little 'reward', and you'll regard your friends who are still in the trap with genuine pity and wonder why they cannot see the point.

However, if you go on kidding yourself that the cigarette was a genuine reward or that you need a substitute to take its place, you will feel deprived and miserable, and the chances are that you'll end up smoking again. If you need a genuine break, as housewives, teachers, doctors and other workers do, you'll soon be enjoying that break even more because you won't have to choke yourself.

Remember, you don't need a substitute. Those pangs are a craving for poison and will soon be gone. Let that be your prop for the next few days. *Enjoy* ridding your body of poison and your mind of slavery and dependence.

If, because your appetite is better, you eat more at main meals and put on a couple of pounds during the next few days, don't worry about it. When you experience the 'moment of revelation' that I describe later, you will have confidence, and you'll find that any problem you have that is capable of being solved by positive thinking you will be able to solve, including eating habits. But what you mustn't do is to start picking between meals. If you do, you will get fat and miserable and you will never know when you've kicked the weed. You'll just be moving the problem instead of getting rid of it.

38

Should I Avoid Temptation Situations?

I have been categorical in my advice so far and would ask you to treat this advice as instruction rather than suggestion. I am categorical, first, because there are sound, practical reasons for my advice and, second, because those reasons have been backed up by tens of thousands of case studies.

On the question of whether or not to try to avoid temptation during the withdrawal period, I regret that I cannot be categorical. Each smoker will need to decide for himself. I can, however, make what I hope will be helpful suggestions.

I repeat that it is fear that keeps us smoking all our lives, and this fear consists of two distinct phases.

1. How can I survive without a cigarette?

This fear is the panic feeling that smokers get when they are out late at night and their cigarettes begin to run out. The fear isn't caused by withdrawal pangs but is the psychological fear of dependency – you cannot survive without a cigarette. It reaches its height when you are smoking your last cigarette; at that time your withdrawal pangs are at their lowest.

It is the fear of the unknown, the sort of fear that people have when they are learning to dive. The diving board is one foot high but seems six feet high. The water is six feet deep but appears one foot deep. It takes courage to launch yourself. You are convinced you are going to smash your head. The launching is the hardest part. If you can find the courage to do it, the rest is easy.

This explains why many otherwise strong-willed smokers either have never attempted to stop or can survive only a few hours when they do. In fact, there are some smokers on about twenty a day who, when they decide to stop, actually smoke their next cigarette more quickly than if they had not decided to stop. The decision causes panic, which is stressful. This is one of the occasions when the brain triggers the instruction: 'Have a cigarette', but now you can't have one. You are being deprived – more stress. The trigger starts again – quickly the fuse blows and you light up.

Don't worry. That panic is just psychological. It is the fear that you are dependent. The beautiful truth is that you are not, even when you are still addicted to nicotine. Do not panic. Just trust me and launch yourself.

2. The second phase of fear is longer term. It involves the fear that certain situations in the future will not be enjoyable without a cigarette or that you will not be able to cope with a trauma without the cigarette. Don't worry. If you can launch yourself you will find the opposite to be the case.

The avoidance of temptation itself falls into two main categories.

1. 'I will keep my cigarettes available, although I will not smoke them. I will feel more confident knowing they are there.'

I find the failure rate with people who do this is far higher than with people who discard them. I believe this is due mainly to the fact that if you have a bad moment during the withdrawal period, it is easy to light up a readily available cigarette. If you have the indignity of having to go out and buy a packet you are more likely to overcome the temptation, and in any event the pang will probably have passed before you get to the tobacconist's.

However, I believe the main reason for the higher failure rate in these cases is that the smoker does not feel completely committed to stopping in the first place. Remember the two essentials to succeed are:

Certainty and 'Isn't it marvellous that I do not need to smoke any more?'

In either case, why on earth do you need cigarettes? If you still feel the need to keep cigarettes on your person, I would suggest that you re-read the book first. It means that something hasn't gelled.

2. 'Should I avoid stressful or social occasions during the withdrawal period?'

My advice is, yes, try to avoid stressful situations. There is no sense in putting undue pressure on yourself.

In the case of social events my advice is the reverse. No, go out and enjoy yourself straight away. You do not need cigarettes even while you are still addicted to nicotine. Go to a party, and rejoice in the fact that you do not have to smoke. It will quickly prove to you the beautiful truth that life is so much better without cigarettes – and just think how much better it will be when the little monster has left your body, together with all that poison.

39 The Moment of Revelation

The moment of revelation usually takes place about three weeks after a smoker stops. The sky appears to become brighter, and it is the moment when the brainwashing ends completely, when, instead of telling yourself you do not need to smoke, you suddenly realize that the last thread is broken and you can enjoy the rest of your life without ever needing to smoke again. It is also usually from this point that you start looking at other smokers as objects of pity.

Smokers using the Willpower Method do not normally experience this moment because, although they are glad to be ex-smokers, they go through life believing they are making a sacrifice.

The more you smoked, the more marvellous this moment is, and it lasts a lifetime.

I consider I have been very fortunate in this life and had some wonderful moments, but the most wonderful of all was that moment of revelation. With all the other highlights of my life, although I can remember they were happy times, I can never recapture the actual feeling. I can never get over the joy of not having to smoke any more. If ever I am feeling low and need a boost nowadays, I just think how lovely it is not to be hooked on that awful weed. Half the people who contact me after they have kicked the weed say exactly the same thing, that it was the most marvellous event of their lives. Ah! What pleasure you have to come!

With an additional twenty years' feedback, both from the book and from my clinics, I have learned that in most cases the moment of revelation occurs not after three weeks as stated above, but within a few days.

In my own case it happened before I'd extinguished my last cigarette, and on many occasions in my early consultancy sessions, during the one-to-one period, before I'd even got to the end of a session, smokers would say something like: 'You needn't say another word, Allen. I can see it all so clearly, I know I'll never smoke again.' In the group sessions I've learned to tell when it happens without individual smokers saying anything. From the letters I receive I'm also aware that it frequently happens with the book.

Ideally if you follow all the instructions and understand the psychology completely, it should happen to you immediately.

Nowadays at my clinics we say to smokers that it takes about five days for the noticeable physical withdrawal to go and about three weeks for an ex-smoker to get completely free. In one way I dislike giving such guidelines. It can cause two problems. The first is that I put in people's minds the suggestion that they will have to suffer for between five days and three weeks. The second is that the ex-smoker tends to think, 'If I can survive for five days or three weeks, I can expect a real boost at the end of that period.' However, he may have five pleasant days or three pleasant weeks, followed by one of those disastrous days that strike both non-smokers and smokers, which have nothing to do with smoking but are caused by other factors in our lives. There our ex-smoker is, waiting for the moment of revelation, and what he experiences is depression instead. It could destroy his confidence.

If I don't give any guidelines, however, the ex-smoker can spend the rest of his life waiting for nothing to happen. I suspect that this is what happens to the vast majority of smokers who stop when using the Willpower Method.

At one time I was tempted to say that revelation should happen immediately. But if I did that and it didn't happen immediately, the ex-smoker would lose confidence and would think it was never going to happen.

People often ask me about the significance of the five days and three weeks. Are they just periods that I've drawn out of the blue? No. They are obviously not definite dates, but they reflect an accumulation of feedback over the years. About five days after stopping is when the ex-smoker ceases to have smoking as the main occupation of his mind. Most ex-smokers experience the moment of revelation around this period. What usually happens is you are in one of those stressful or social situations that once you couldn't cope with or enjoy without a cigarette. You suddenly realize that not only are you enjoying or coping with it but the thought of having a cigarette has not even occurred to you. From that point on it is usually plain sailing. That's when you know you are free.

I have noticed from my previous attempts using the Willpower Method, and from feedback from other smokers, that around the three-week period is when most serious attempts to stop smoking fail. I believe that what usually happens is that after about three weeks you sense that you have lost the desire to smoke. You need to prove this to yourself, and you light a cigarette. It tastes weird. You've proved you have kicked it. But you've also put fresh nicotine into your body, and nicotine is what your body has been craving for three weeks. As soon as you extinguish that cigarette, the nicotine starts to leave your body. Now a little voice is saying, 'You haven't kicked it. You want another one.' You don't light another one straight away because you don't want to get hooked again. You allow a safe period to pass. When you are next tempted you are able to say to yourself, 'But I didn't get hooked again, so there's no harm in having another.' You are already on your way down the slippery slope.

The key to the problem is not to wait for the moment of revelation but to realize that once you extinguish that last cigarette it is finished. You've already done all you need to do. You've cut off the supply of nicotine. No force on earth can prevent you from being free unless you mope about it or wait for revelation. Go and enjoy life; cope with it right from the start. That way you'll soon experience the moment.

40 The Final Cigarette

Having decided on your timing, you are now ready to smoke that last cigarette. Before you do so, check on the two essentials:

1. Do you feel certain of success?
2. Have you a feeling of doom and gloom or a sense of excitement that you are about to achieve something marvellous?

If you have any doubts, re-read the book first. If you still have doubts, obtain a copy of *The Only Way to Stop Smoking Permanently* (ONLYWAY) published by Penguin or contact your nearest Allen Carr's Easyway clinic, details of which are listed at the end.

Remember that you never decided to fall into the smoking trap. But that trap is designed to enslave you for life. In order to escape you need to make the positive decision that you are about to smoke your final cigarette.

Remember, the only reason that you have read this book so far is because you would dearly love to escape. So make that positive decision now. Make a solemn vow that when you extinguish that final cigarette, whether you find it easy or difficult, you will never smoke another.

Perhaps you are worried that you have made this vow several times in the past but are still smoking, or that you will have to go through some awful trauma. Have no fear, the worst thing that can possibly happen is that you fail, and so you have absolutely nothing to lose and so much to gain.

But stop even thinking about failure. The beautiful truth is that it is not only ridiculously easy to quit but you can actually enjoy the process. This time you are going to use EASYWAY! All you need to do is to follow the simple instructions that I'm about to give you:

1. Make the solemn vow now and mean it.
2. Smoke that final cigarette consciously, inhale the filth deeply into your lungs and ask yourself where the pleasure is.
3. When you extinguish it, do so not with a feeling of: I must never smoke another, or I'm not allowed to smoke another, but with the feeling: Isn't it great! I'm free! I'm no longer the slave of nicotine! I don't ever have to put these filthy things in my mouth again.
4. Be aware that for a few days, there will be a little nicotine saboteur inside your stomach. You might only know the feeling: 'I want a cigarette.' At times I refer to that little nicotine monster as the slight physical craving for nicotine. Strictly this is incorrect, and it is important you understand why. Because it takes about three weeks for that little monster to die, ex-smokers believe that the little monster will continue to crave cigarettes after the final cigarette has been extinguished, and that they must therefore use willpower to resist the temptation during this period. This is not so. The body doesn't crave nicotine. Only the brain craves nicotine. If you do get that feeling of 'I want a cigarette' over the next few days, your brain has a simple

choice. Either it can interpret that feeling for what it actually is – an empty insecure feeling started by the first cigarette and perpetuated by every subsequent one, and you can say to yourself: YIPPEE I'M A NON-SMOKER! Or you can start craving for a cigarette and suffer it for the rest of your life.

Just think for a moment. Wouldn't that be an incredibly stupid thing to do? To say, 'I never want to smoke again,' then spend the rest of your life saying 'I'd love a cigarette.' That's what smokers who use the Willpower Method do. No wonder they feel so miserable. They spend the rest of their lives desperately moping for something that they desperately hope they will never have. No wonder so few of them succeed and the few that do never feel completely free.

5. It is only the doubting and the waiting that makes it difficult to quit. So never doubt your decision, you know it's the correct decision. If you begin to doubt it, you will put yourself into a no-win situation. You will be miserable if you crave a cigarette but can't have one. You will be even more miserable if you do have one. No matter what system you are using, what is it that you are trying to achieve when you quit smoking? Never to smoke again? No! Many ex-smokers do that but go through the rest of their lives feeling deprived. What is the real difference between smokers and non-smokers? Non-smokers have no need or desire to smoke, they do not crave cigarettes and do not need to exercise willpower in order not to smoke. That's what you are trying to achieve, and it is completely within your power to achieve it. You don't have to wait to stop craving cigarettes or to become a non-smoker. You do it the moment you extinguish that

final cigarette, you have cut off the supply of nicotine: YOU ARE ALREADY A HAPPY NON-SMOKER!

And you will remain a happy non-smoker provided:

1. You never doubt your decision.
2. You don't wait to become a non-smoker. If you do, you will merely be waiting for nothing to happen, which will create a phobia.
3. You don't try not to think about smoking or wait for the 'moment of revelation' to come. Either way you will merely create a phobia.
4. You don't use substitutes.
5. You see all other smokers as they really are and pity them rather than envy them.
6. Whether there be good days or bad days, you don't change your life just because you've quit smoking. If you do you will be making a genuine sacrifice and there is no need to. Remember, you haven't given up living. You haven't given up anything. On the contrary, you've cured yourself from an awful disease and escaped from an insidious prison. As the days go by and your health, both physical and mental improves, the highs will appear higher and the lows less low than when you were a smoker.
7. Whenever you think about smoking either during the next few days or the rest of your life, you think: YIPPEE, I'M A NON-SMOKER!

41

A Final Warning

No smoker, given the chance of going back to the time before he became hooked with the knowledge he has now, would opt to start. Many of the smokers who consult me are convinced that if I could only help them stop, they would never dream of smoking again, and yet thousands of smokers quit successfully for many years and lead perfectly happy lives, only to get trapped once again.

I trust that this book will help you to find it relatively easy to stop smoking. But be warned: smokers who find it easy to stop find it easy to start again.

DO NOT FALL INTO THIS TRAP

No matter how long you have stopped or how confident you are that you will never become hooked again, make it a rule of life not to smoke for any reason. Resist the millions of pounds that the tobacco companies spend on promotion, and remember they are pushing the Number 1 killer drug and poison. You wouldn't be tempted to try heroin; and cigarettes kill hundreds of thousands more people than heroin does.

Remember, that first cigarette will do nothing for you.

You will have no withdrawal pangs to relieve, and it will taste awful. What it will do is to put nicotine into your body, and a little voice at the back of your mind will be saying, 'You want another one.' Then you have got the choice of being miserable for a while or starting the whole filthy chain again.

42 Feedback

Since the original publication of this book I now have twenty years' feedback, not only from my own consultations, but also from my worldwide clinic network and from the book itself which has been translated into more than 27 languages. Originally it was a struggle. My method was pooh-poohed by the so-called experts. Now smokers from all over the world attend my clinics, and more members of the medical profession attend them than members of any other profession. The book is regarded in the UK as the most effective aid for stopping smoking, and its reputation is rapidly spreading throughout the rest of the world.

I'm not a do-gooder. My war — which, I emphasize, is not against smokers but against the nicotine trap — I wage for the purely selfish reason that I enjoy it. Every time I hear of a smoker escaping from the prison I get a feeling of great pleasure, even when it has nothing to do with me. You can imagine also the immense pleasure I obtain from the tens of thousands of grateful letters and emails that I have received over the years.

There has also been considerable frustration. The frustration is caused mainly by two main categories of smoker. First, in spite of the warning in the previous chapter, I am disturbed by the number of smokers who find it easy to stop, yet get hooked again and find they can't succeed the next time. This applies not only to readers of the book but also to my consultations.

A man telephoned me a few years ago. He was very distraught; in fact, he was crying. He said, 'I'll pay you £1,000 if you can help me stop for a week. I know if I can just survive a week, I'll be able to do it.' I told him that I charge a fixed fee and that was all he need pay. He attended a group session and, much to his surprise, found it easy to stop. He sent me a very nice thank-you letter.

Practically the last thing I say to ex-smokers leaving my sessions is: 'Remember, you must never smoke another cigarette.' This particular man said, 'Have no fear, Allen. If I manage to stop, I'll definitely never smoke again.'

I could tell that the warning hadn't really registered. I said, 'I know you feel like that at the moment, but how will you feel six months on?'

He said, 'Allen, I will never smoke again.'

About a year later there was another phone call. 'Allen, I had a small cigar at Christmas, and now I'm back on forty cigarettes a day.'

I said, 'Do you remember when you first phoned? You hated it so much you were going to pay me £1,000 if you could stop for a week. Do you remember you promised me you would never smoke again?'

'I know. I'm a fool.'

It's like finding someone up to his neck in a bog and about to go under. You help pull him out. He is grateful to you and then, six months later, dives straight back into the bog.

Ironically, when this man attended a subsequent session

he said, 'Can you believe it? I offered to pay my son £1,000 if he hadn't smoked by his twenty-first birthday. I paid up. He's now twenty-two and puffing away like a chimney. I can't believe he could be so stupid.'

I said, 'I don't see how you can call him stupid. At least he avoided the trap for twenty-two years, and he doesn't know the misery he's in for. You knew it as well as anyone and survived only a year.'

If re-reading EASYWAY doesn't help, read ONLYWAY or contact your nearest EASYWAY clinic. Smokers who find it easy to stop and start again pose a special problem. However, when you get free PLEASE, PLEASE, DON'T MAKE THE SAME MISTAKE. Smokers believe that such people start again because they are still hooked and are missing the cigarette. In fact, they find stopping so easy that they lose their fear of smoking. They think, 'I can have an odd cigarette. Even if I do get hooked again, I'll find it easy to stop again.'

I'm afraid it just doesn't work that way. It's easy to stop smoking, but it's impossible to try to control the addiction. The only thing that is essential to becoming a non-smoker is *not to smoke*.

The other category of smokers that causes me frustration is those who are just too frightened to make the attempt to stop or, when they do, find it a great struggle. The main difficulties appear to be the following:

1. **Fear of failure** There is no disgrace in failure, but not to try is plain stupidity. Look at it this way – you're hiding from nothing. The worst thing that can happen is that you fail, in which case you are no worse off than you are now. Just think how wonderful it would be to succeed. If you

don't make the attempt, you have already guaranteed failure.

2. **Fear of panic and of being miserable.** Don't worry about it. Just think: what awful thing could happen to you if you never smoked another cigarette? Absolutely nothing. Terrible things will happen if you do. In any case, the panic is caused by cigarettes and will soon be gone. The greatest gain is to be rid of that fear. Do you really believe that smokers are prepared to have their arms and legs removed for the pleasure they get from smoking? If you find yourself feeling panicky, deep breathing will help. If you are with other people and they are getting you down, go away from them. Escape to the garage or an empty office or wherever.

If you feel like crying, don't be ashamed. Crying is nature's way of relieving tension. No one has ever had a good cry without feeling better afterwards. One of the awful things we do to young boys is to teach them not to cry. You see them trying to fight the tears back, but watch the jaw grinding away. As Britons, we teach ourselves to keep a stiff upper lip, not to show any emotions. We are meant to show emotions, not to try to bottle them up inside us. Scream or shout or have a tantrum. Kick a cardboard box or filing cabinet. Regard your struggle as a boxing match that you cannot lose.

No one can stop time. Every moment that passes that little monster inside you is dying. Enjoy your inevitable victory.

3. **Not following the instructions.** Incredibly, some smokers say to me, 'Your method just didn't work for me.' They then describe how they ignored not only one instruction but practically all of them. (For clarification I

will summarize these in the check-list at the end of the chapter.)

4. **Misunderstanding instructions** The chief problems appear to be these.

(a) 'I can't stop thinking about smoking.' Of course you can't, and if you try, you will create a phobia and be miserable. It's like trying to get to sleep at night; the more you try, the harder it becomes. I think about smoking 90 per cent of my life. It's what you are thinking that's important. If you are thinking, 'Oh, I'd love a cigarette,' or 'When will I be free?' you'll be miserable. If you are thinking, 'YIPPEE! I am free!' you'll be happy.

(b) 'When will the little physical monster die?' The nicotine leaves your body very rapidly. But it is impossible to tell when your body will cease to suffer from the slight physical sensation of nicotine withdrawal. That empty, insecure feeling is identical to normal hunger, depression or stress. All the cigarette does is to increase the level of it. This is why smokers who stop by using the Willpower Method are never quite sure whether they've kicked it. Even after the body has ceased to suffer from nicotine withdrawal, if they suffer normal hunger or stress, their brain is still saying, 'That means you want a cigarette.' The point is you don't have to wait for the nicotine craving to go; it is so slight that we don't even know it's there. We know it only as feeling 'I want a cigarette.' When you leave the dentist, do you wait for your jaw to stop aching? Of course you don't. You get on with your life. Even though your jaw's still aching, you are elated.

(c) Waiting for the moment of revelation. If you wait for it, you are just causing another phobia. I once stopped for three weeks on the Willpower Method. I met an old school friend and ex-smoker. He said, 'How are you getting on?'

I said, I've survived three weeks.'

He said, 'What do you mean, you've survived three weeks?'

I said, 'I've gone three weeks without a cigarette.'

He said, 'What are you going to do? *Survive* the rest of your life? What are you waiting for? You've done it. You're a non-smoker.'

I thought, 'He's absolutely right. What am I waiting for?' Unfortunately, because I didn't fully understand the nature of the trap at that time, I was soon back in it, but the point was noted. You become a non-smoker when you extinguish your last cigarette. The important thing is to be a happy non-smoker from the start.

(d) 'I am still craving cigarettes.' Then you are being very stupid. How can you claim, 'I want to be a non-smoker,' and then say, 'I want a cigarette'? That's a contradiction. If you say, 'I want a cigarette,' you are saying, 'I want to be a smoker.' Non-smokers don't want to smoke cigarettes. You already know what you really want to be, so stop punishing yourself.

(e) 'I've opted out of life.' Why? All you have to do is stop choking yourself. You don't have to stop living. Look, it's as simple as this. For the next few days you'll have a slight trauma in your life. Your body will suffer the almost imperceptible aggravation of withdrawal from nicotine. Now, bear this in mind: you are no worse off than you were. This is what you have been suffering the whole of your smoking life, every time you have been asleep or in a church, supermarket or library. It didn't seem to bother you when you were a smoker, and if you don't stop, you'll go on suffering this distress for the rest of your life. Cigarettes don't make meals or drinks or social occasions; they ruin them. Even while your body is still craving nicotine, meals and social occasions are marvellous. Life is marvellous. Go to social functions, even if there are twenty smokers there. Remember that you are not being deprived; they are. Every one of them would love to be in your position. Enjoy being the prima donna and the centre of attention. Stopping smoking is a wonderful conversation point, particularly when smokers see that you are happy and cheerful. They'll think that you are incredible. The important point is that you'll be enjoying life right from the start. There's no need to envy them. They'll be envying you.

(f) 'I am miserable and irritable.' That is because you haven't followed my instructions. Find out which one it is. Some people understand and believe everything I say but still start off with a feeling of doom and gloom, as if something terrible were happening. You are doing not only what you'd like to do but what every smoker on the planet would like to do. With any method of stopping, what the ex-smoker is trying to achieve is a certain frame of mind, so that whenever he thinks about smoking he says to himself, 'YIPPEE! I'M FREE!' If that's your object, why wait? Start off in that frame of mind and never lose it. The rest of the book is designed to make you understand why there is no alternative.

The Check-list

If you follow these simple instructions, you cannot fail.

1. Make a solemn vow that you will never, ever, smoke, chew or suck anything that contains nicotine, and stick to your vow.
2. Get this clear in your mind: there is absolutely nothing to *give up*. By that I don't mean simply that you will be better off as a non-smoker (you've known that all your life); nor do I mean that although there is no rational reason why you smoke, you must get some form of pleasure or crutch from it or you wouldn't do it. What I mean is, there is no genuine pleasure or crutch in smoking. It is just an illusion, like banging your head against a wall to make it pleasant when you stop.
3. There is no such thing as a confirmed smoker. You are just one of the millions who have fallen for this subtle trap. Like millions of other ex-smokers who once thought they couldn't escape, you have escaped.
4. If at any time in your life you were to weigh up the pros and cons of smoking, the conclusion would always be, a dozen times over, 'Stop doing it. You are a fool.' Nothing will ever change that. It always has been that way, and it always will be. Having made what you know to be the correct decision, don't ever torture yourself by doubting it.
5. Don't try *not* to think about smoking or worry that you are thinking about it constantly. But whenever you do think about it – whether it be today, tomorrow or the rest of your life – think, 'YIPPEE! I'M A NON-SMOKER!'
6. DO NOT use any form of substitute.
   DO NOT keep your own cigarettes.

DO NOT avoid other smokers.
DO NOT change your lifestyle in any way purely because you've stopped smoking.

    If you follow the above instructions, you will soon experience the moment of revelation. But:

7. Don't wait for that moment to come. Just get on with your life. Enjoy the highs and cope with the lows. You will find that in no time at all the moment will arrive.

43 Help the Smoker Left on the Sinking Ship

Smokers are panicking nowadays. They sense that there is a change in society. Smoking is now regarded as thoroughly antisocial, even by smokers themselves. They also sense that the whole thing is coming to an end. Millions of smokers are now stopping, and all smokers are conscious of this fact.

Every time a smoker leaves the sinking ship, the ones left on it feel more miserable. Every smoker instinctively knows that it is ridiculous to pay good money for dried leaves rolled up in paper, to set light to them and to breathe cancer-triggering tar into his lungs. If you still don't think it is silly, try sticking a burning cigarette in your ear and ask yourself what the difference is. Just one. You cannot get the nicotine that way. If you can stop sticking cigarettes in your mouth, you won't need the nicotine.

Smokers cannot find a rational reason for smoking, but if someone else is doing it, they do not feel quite so silly.

Smokers blatantly lie about their smoking, not only to others but to themselves. They have to. The brainwashing is essential if they are to retain some self-respect. They feel the need to justify their smoking, not only to themselves but also to non-smokers. They are therefore forever advertising the illusory advantages of smoking.

If a smoker stops on the Willpower Method, he still feels deprived and tends to become a moaner. All this does is to confirm to other smokers how right they are to keep smoking.

If the ex-smoker succeeds in getting free, he is grateful that he no longer has to go through life choking himself or wasting money. What's more, he has no need to justify himself, he doesn't sit there saying how marvellous it is not to be smoking. He will do that only if he is asked, and smokers won't ask that question. They wouldn't like the answer. Remember, it is fear that keeps them smoking, and they would rather keep their heads in the sand.

The only time they ask that question is when it is time to stop.

Help the smoker. Remove these fears. Tell him how marvellous it is not to have to go through life choking yourself, how lovely it is to wake up in the morning feeling fit and healthy instead of wheezing and coughing, how wonderful it is to be free of slavery, to be able to enjoy the whole of your life, to be rid of those awful black shadows. Or, better still, get him to read the book.

It is essential not to belittle the smoker by indicating that he is polluting the atmosphere or is in some way unclean. There is a common conception that the ex-smoker is the worst in this respect. I believe this conception has some substance, and I think this is due to the Willpower Method of stopping. Because the ex-smoker, although he has quit, retains part of the brainwashing, part of him still believes that he has made a sacrifice. He feels vulnerable, and his natural defensive mechanism is to attack the smoker. This may help the ex-smoker, but it does nothing to help the smoker. All it does is put his back up, make him feel even more wretched and consequently make his need for a cigarette even greater.

Although the change in society's attitude to smoking is the main reason why millions of smokers are quitting, it doesn't make it easier for them to do so. In fact, it makes it a great deal harder. Most smokers nowadays believe they are stopping mainly for health reasons. This is not strictly true. Although the enormous health risk is obviously the chief reason for quitting, smokers have been killing themselves for years and it has made not the slightest difference. The main reason why smokers are stopping is because society is beginning to see smoking for what it actually is: filthy drug addiction. The enjoyment was always an illusion; this attitude removes this illusion, so that the smoker is left with nothing.

When the complete ban on smoking in London's Underground system was first introduced it was a classic example of the smoker's dilemma. The smoker either takes the attitude: 'OK, if I can't smoke on the train, I'll find another means of travel,' which does no good but merely loses London Transport valuable revenue, or he says: 'Fine, it will help me cut down on my smoking.' The result of this is that instead of smoking one or two cigarettes on the train, neither of which he would have enjoyed, he abstains for an hour. During this enforced period of abstinence, however, not only will he be mentally deprived and waiting for his reward but his body will have been craving nicotine – and, oh, how precious that cigarette will be when he is eventually allowed to light up. How much worse life must be for a smoker with the introduction of full scale smoking bans in public places.

Enforced abstinences do not actually cut down the intake because the smoker just indulges himself in more cigarettes when he is eventually allowed to smoke. All it does is to ingrain in the smoker's mind how precious cigarettes are and how dependent he is upon them.

I think the most insidious aspect of this enforced abstinence is its effect on pregnant women. We allow unfortunate teenagers to be bombarded with massive brainwashing that gets them hooked in the first place. Then, at what is probably the most stressful period in their lives, when in their deluded minds they need cigarettes most of all, the medical profession blackmails them into giving up because of the harm they are causing the baby. Many are unable to do so and are forced, through no fault of their own, to suffer a guilt complex for the rest of their lives. Many of them succeed and are pleased to do so, thinking, 'Fine, I will do this for the baby and after nine months I will be cured anyway.' Then comes the pain and fear of labour, followed by the biggest 'high' of their lives. The pain and fear are over, and the beautiful, new baby has arrived and the old trigger mechanism comes into operation. Part of the brainwashing is still there, and almost before the cord has been cut, the mother has a cigarette in her mouth. The elation of the occasion blocks the foul taste from her mind. She has no intention of becoming hooked again. 'Just the one cigarette.' Too late! She is already hooked. Nicotine has got into her body again. The old craving will start.

It is strange that although heroin addicts are criminals in law, our society's attitude is quite rightly 'What can we do to help the pathetic individuals?' Let us adopt the same attitude to the poor smoker. He is not smoking because he wants to but because he thinks he has to, and, unlike the heroin addict, he usually has to suffer years and years of mental and physical torture. We always say a quick death is better than a slow one, so do not envy the poor smoker. He deserves your pity.

44

Advice to Non-smokers

Help Get Your Smoking Friends or Relatives to Read This Book

First study the contents of this book and try to put yourself in the place of the smoker.

Do not force him to read this book or try to stop him smoking by telling him he is ruining his health or wasting his money. He already knows this better than you do. Smokers do not smoke because they enjoy it or because they want to. They only tell themselves and other people this in order to retain self-respect. They smoke because they feel dependent on cigarettes, because they think that the cigarette relaxes them and gives them courage and confidence and that life will never be enjoyable without a cigarette. If you try to force a smoker to stop, he feels like a trapped animal and wants his cigarette even more. This may turn him into a secret smoker and in his mind the cigarette will become even more precious (see chapter 26).

Instead, concentrate on the other side of the coin. Get him into the company of ex-smokers (there are 15 million of them in Britain alone). Get them to tell the smoker how they too thought they were hooked for life and how much better life is as a non-smoker.

Once you have got him believing that he can stop, his mind will start opening. Then start explaining the delusion created by withdrawal pangs. Not only are the cigarettes not giving him a boost but it is they that are destroying his confidence and making him irritable and unrelaxed.

He should now be ready to read this book himself. He will be expecting to read pages and pages about lung cancer, heart diseases, etc. Explain that the approach is completely different and that references to illness are just a small fraction of the material in the book.

Help During the Withdrawal Period

Whether the ex-smoker is suffering or not, assume that he is. Do not try to minimize his suffering by telling him it is easy to stop; he can do that himself. Instead keep telling him how proud you are, how much better he is looking, how much sweeter he smells, how much easier his breathing is. It is particularly important to keep doing this. When a smoker makes an attempt to stop, the euphoria of the attempt and the attention he gets from friends and colleagues can help him along. However, they tend to forget quickly, so keep that praise going.

Because he is not talking about smoking, you may think he has forgotten about it and don't want to remind him. Usually the complete opposite is the case with the Willpower Method, as the ex-smoker tends to be obsessed by nothing else. So do not be frightened to bring the subject up, and keep praising him; he will tell you if he doesn't want you to remind him of smoking.

Go out of your way to relieve him of pressures during the withdrawal period. Try to think of ways of making his life interesting and enjoyable.

This can also be a trying period for non-smokers. If one member of a group is irritable, it can cause general misery all round. So anticipate this if the ex-smoker is feeling irritable. He may well take it out on you, but do not retaliate; it is at this time that he needs your praise and sympathy the most. If you are feeling irritable yourself, try not to show it.

One of the tricks I used to play when trying to give up with the aid of the Willpower Method was to get into a tantrum, hoping that my wife or friends would say, 'I cannot bear to see you suffering like this. For goodness' sake, have a cigarette.' The smoker then does not lose face, as he isn't 'giving in' – he has been instructed. If the ex-smoker uses this ploy, on no account encourage him to smoke. Instead say, 'If that is what cigarettes do to you, thank goodness you will soon be free. How marvellous that you had the courage and sense to give up.'

Finale: Help End This Scandal

In my opinion, cigarette smoking is the biggest scandal in society, including nuclear weapons.

Surely the very basis of civilization, the reason why the human species has advanced so far, is that we are capable of communicating our knowledge and experiences not only to each other but to future generations. Even the lower species find it necessary to warn their offspring of the pitfalls in life.

If nuclear weapons do not go off, there is no problem. The people who advocate nuclear armaments can carry on saying smugly, 'They are keeping the peace.' If they do go off, they will solve the smoking problem and every other problem, and a bonus for the politicians is that there will be nobody around to say, 'You were wrong' (I wonder if this is why they support nuclear weapons).

However, much as I disagree with nuclear weapons, at least such decisions are made in good faith, in the genuine belief that they help mankind, whereas with smoking, the true facts are known. Maybe during World War II people genuinely believed that cigarettes gave you courage and confidence. Today the authorities know that is a fallacy. Just look at cigarette marketing nowadays. They make no claims about relaxation or pleasure. The only claims they make are about the quality of the tobacco. Why should we be worried about the quality of a poison?

The sheer hypocrisy is incredible. As a society we get uptight about cocaine and heroin addiction. Compared with smoking, these problems are tiny. Sixty per cent of the population have been addicted to nicotine, and many of them spend money they can ill afford on cigarettes. Tens of thousands of people have their lives ruined every year because they become hooked. Smoking is by far the biggest killer in society and yet the biggest vested interest is our own Treasury. It makes more than £8,000,000,000 every year out of the misery of nicotine addicts, and the tobacco empires are allowed to spend £120,000,000 per year on marketing and publicity for their filth.

How clever that cigarette companies print that health warning on packets, and our government spends a pittance on TV campaigns involving cancer scares, bad breath and legs being chopped off, and they justify themselves by saying, 'We have warned you of the danger. It is your choice.' The smoker doesn't have the choice any more than the heroin addict does. Smokers do not decide to become hooked; they are lured into a subtle trap. If smokers had the choice, the only smokers tomorrow morning would be the youngsters starting out believing they could stop any time they wanted to.

Why the phoney standards? Why are heroin addicts seen as criminals, yet can register as addicts and get free heroin and proper medical treatment to help get off it? Just try registering as a nicotine addict. You cannot get cigarettes at cost. You have to pay three times the true value and every Budget Day you will be screwed further by the Government. As if the smoker hadn't got troubles enough!

If you go to your doctor for help, either he will tell you,

'Stop doing it, it's killing you,' which you already know, or he will prescribe another form of nicotine addiction that will cost you a prescription fee and actually contains the drug you are trying to kick.

Scare campaigns do not help smokers to stop. They make it harder. All they do is to frighten smokers, which makes them want to smoke even more. It doesn't even prevent teenagers from becoming hooked. Teenagers know that cigarettes kill, but they also know one cigarette will not do it. Because smoking is so prevalent, sooner or later the teenager, through social pressures or curiosity, will try just one cigarette. And *because* it tastes so awful, he will probably become hooked.

Why do we allow this scandal to go on? Why doesn't our government come out with a proper campaign? Why doesn't it tell us that nicotine is a drug and a killer poison, that it does not relax you or give you confidence but destroys your nerves and that it can take just one cigarette to become hooked?

I remember reading H G Wells's *The Time Machine*. The book describes an incident in the distant future in which a man falls into a river. His companions merely sit around on the bank like cattle, oblivious to his cries of desperation. I found that incident inhuman and very disturbing. I find the general apathy of our society to the smoking problem very similar. In particular, I find it disturbing that in 2006 the Government and the medical and scientific establishments still ignored my method of stopping smoking in favour of using vast sums of taxpayers' money to create future generations of nicotine addicts using not just cigarettes but nicotine patches, gums, and all sorts of other new nicotine delivery products.

Why do we allow society to subject healthy young teen-agers, youngsters whose lives were complete before they started smoking, to go on paying through the nose for the rest of their lives just for the privilege of destroying themselves mentally and physically in a lifetime of slavery, a lifetime of filth and disease?

You may feel that I overdramatize the facts. Not so. My father was cut down in his early fifties because of cigarette smoking. He was a strong man and might still have been alive today.

I believe I was within an inch of dying during my forties, although my death would have been attributed to a brain haemorrhage rather than to cigarette smoking. I now spend my life being consulted by people who have been crippled by the disease or are in the last stages. And, if you care to think about it, you probably know of many too.

There is a wind of change in society. A snowball has started that I hope this book will help turn into an avalanche.

You too can help by spreading the message.

IN THE UK, THE GOVERNMENT IS SPENDING MILLIONS OF POUNDS OF TAXPAYERS' MONEY ON SO-CALLED NICOTINE REPLACEMENT THERAPY (NRT) AND IS IGNORING ALLEN CARR'S EASYWAY. YOU CANNOT CURE NICOTINE ADDICTION BY GIVING THE ADDICT NICOTINE. CURRENT GOVERNMENT POLICY IS PERPETUATING NICOTINE ADDICTION AT THE EXPENSE OF THE TAXPAYER AND THE ONLY WINNERS ARE THE PHARMACEUTICAL COMPANIES MAKING NRT WHO ARE NOW COMPETING WITH THE TOBACCO COMPANIES TO SUPPLY THE NICOTINE-ADDICTED MARKET. WHEREVER YOU ARE IN THE WORLD, IF YOU FEEL YOU HAVE BENEFITTED FROM ALLEN CARR'S EASYWAY METHOD, CAN SEE THE ABSURDITY OF SUPPLYING NICOTINE AT TAXPAYERS' EXPENSE AND WOULD LIKE TO HELP OTHERS BY MAKING ALLEN CARR'S EASYWAY AVAILABLE ON YOUR NATIONAL HEALTH SERVICE (IF YOU HAVE ONE), THEN PLEASE WRITE TO YOUR DOCTOR, THE POLITICIANS, THE MEDICAL ESTABLISHMENT, THE NEWSPAPERS, THE TV AND RADIO STATIONS AND OTHER MEDIA IN YOUR COUNTRY AND ON THE INTERNET, DRAWING ATTENTION TO THIS SCANDALOUS SITUATION. YOU CAN MAKE A DIFFERENCE.

Final Warning

You can now enjoy the rest of your life as a happy non-smoker. In order to make sure that you do, you need to follow these simple instructions:

1. Keep this book safely in a place where you can easily refer to it. Do not lose it, lend it out or give it away.

2. If you ever start to envy another smoker, realize that they will be envious of you. You are not being deprived. They are.

3. Remember you did not enjoy being a smoker. That's why you stopped. You do enjoy being a non-smoker.

4. Remember, there is no such thing as just one cigarette.

5. Never doubt your decision never to smoke again. You know it's the correct decision.

6. If you have any difficulties contact your nearest Allen Carr's EASYWAY clinic. You will find a list of these on the following pages.

HELP LINE 0800 389 2115

The team of trained therapists at our UK clinics would be happy to answer any questions or concerns that you may have – so please do not hesitate to call your nearest clinic on the above number if you have any difficulties at all.

Now at last you can say
'YIPPEE! I'M A NON-SMOKER'

You have achieved something really marvellous. Every time we hear of a smoker escaping from the sinking ship, we get a feeling of enormous satisfaction.

It would give us great pleasure to hear that you have freed yourself from the slavery of smoking so please do sign the following, add your comments and send it to:

Allen Carr's EASYWAY, Park House, 14 Pepys Road, London SW20 8NH or email the same information to mail@allencarr.com

YIPPEE! I'M A NON-SMOKER

Signed _____   Date _____

Name _____

Address _____

_____

_____   Postcode _____

Email address _____

Allen Carr's Easyway Clinics

The following pages list contact details for all Allen Carr's Easyway To Stop Smoking Clinics/Centres worldwide where the success rate, based on the three month money back guarantee, is over 90 per cent.

Selected clinics also offer sessions that deal with alcohol and weight issues. Please check with your nearest clinic, which is listed, for details.

Allen Carr's Easyway guarantees that you will find it easy to stop smoking at the clinics or your money back.

ALLEN CARR'S EASYWAY – WORLD-WIDE HEAD OFFICE

Park House
14 Pepys Road
Raynes Park
London SW20 8NH
Telephone: +44 (0)208 944 7761
Email: mail@allencarr.com
Website: www.allencarr.com

WORLDWIDE PRESS OFFICE
Telephone: +44 (0)7970 88 44 52
Email: jd@statacom.net
UK Clinic Information and
    Central Booking Line 0800 389
    2115 (Freephone)

UNITED KINGDOM

LONDON
Park House
14 Pepys Road
Raynes Park
London SW20 8NH

Telephone: 020 8944 7761
Fax: 020 8944 8619
Therapists: John Dicey,
    Sue Bolshaw, Sam Carroll,
    Colleen Dwyer, Crispin Hay,
    Emma Sole, Rob Fielding,
    James Pyper
Email: mail@allencarr.com
Website: www.allencarr.com

AYLESBURY
Telephone: 0800 0197 017
Therapists: Kim Bennett,
    Emma Sole
Email: kim@easywaybucks.co.uk
Website: www.allencarr.com

BELFAST
Telephone: 0845 094 3244
Therapist: Tara Evers-Cheung
Email: tara@easywayni.com
Website: www.allencarr.com

BIRMINGHAM
Telephone and Fax: 0121 423 1227
Therapists: John Dicey,
    Colleen Dwyer, Crispin Hay,
    Rob Fielding
Email: easywayadmin@
    tiscali.co.uk
Website: www.allencarr.com

BOURNEMOUTH
Telephone: 0800 028 7257/01425
    272 757
Therapists: John Dicey,
    Colleen Dwyer, Sam Carroll,
    Emma Sole, James Pyper
Email: easywayadmin@
    tiscali.co.uk
Website: www.allencarr.com

BRIGHTON
Telephone: 0800 028 7257
Therapists: John Dicey,
    Colleen Dwyer, Sam Carroll,
    Emma Sole, James Pyper
Email: easywayadmin@
    tiscali.co.uk
Website: www.allencarr.com

BRISTOL
Telephone: 0117 950 1441
Therapist: Charles Holdsworth
    Hunt
Email: stopsmoking@
    easywaybristol.co.uk
Website: www.allencarr.com

CAMBRIDGE
Telephone: 0800 0197 017
Therapists: Kim Bennett,
    Emma Sole
Email: kim@easywaybucks.co.uk
Website: www.allencarr.com

CARDIFF
Telephone: 0117 950 1441
Therapist: Charles Holdsworth
    Hunt
Email: stopsmoking@
    easywaybristol.co.uk
Website: www.allencarr.com

COVENTRY
Telephone: 0800 321 3007
Therapist: Rob Fielding
Email: info@easyway
    coventry.co.uk
Website: www.allencarr.com

CREWE
Telephone: 01270 501 487
Therapist: Debbie Brewer-West
Email: debbie@easyway2stop
    smoking.co.uk
Website: www.allencarr.com

CUMBRIA
Telephone: 0800 077 6187
Therapist: Mark Keen
Email: mark@easyway
    cumbria.co.uk
Website: www.allencarr.com

DERBY
Telephone: 0800 0197 017
Therapists: Kim Bennett,
    Emma Sole
Email: kim@easywaybucks.co.uk
Website: www.allencarr.com

ESSEX (OPENING SOON)
Telephone: 0800 389 2115
Website: www.allencarr.com

EXETER
Telephone: 0117 950 1441
Therapist: Charles Holdsworth Hunt
Email: stopsmoking@
    easywayexeter.co.uk
Website: www.allencarr.com

HIGH WYCOMBE
Telephone: 0800 0197 017
Therapists: Kim Bennett,
    Emma Sole
Email: kim@easywaybucks.co.uk
Website: www.allencarr.com

IPSWICH
Telephone: 0800 389 2115
Therapists: David Piper and
    Gary Harris
Email: info@easyway
    suffolk.co.uk
Website: www.allencarr.com

KENT
Telephone: 0800 028 7257
Therapists: John Dicey,
    Colleen Dwyer, Sam Carroll,
    Emma Sole, James Pyper
Website: www.allencarr.com

LANCASHIRE
Telephone: 0800 077 6187
Therapist: Mark Keen
Email: mark@easyway
    lancashire.co.uk
Website: www.allencarr.com

LEEDS
Telephone: 0800 804 6796
Therapist: Rob Groves
Email: stopsmoking@easyway
    yorkshire.co.uk
Website: www.allencarr.com

LEICESTER
Telephone: 0800 321 3007
Therapist: Rob Fielding
Email: info@easyway
    leicester.co.uk
Website: www.allencarr.com

LINCOLN
Telephone: 0800 321 3007
Therapist: Rob Fielding
Website: www.allencarr.com

LIVERPOOL
Telephone: 0800 077 6187
Therapist: Mark Keen
Email: mark@easyway
    liverpool.co.uk
Website: www.allencarr.com

MANCHESTER
Telephone: 0800 804 6796
Therapist: Rob Groves
Email: stopsmoking@easyway
    manchester.co.uk
Website: www.allencarr.com

MILTON KEYNES
Telephone: 0800 0197 017
Therapists: Kim Bennett,
    Emma Sole
Email: kim@easywaybucks.co.uk
Website: www.allencarr.com

NEWCASTLE/NORTH EAST
Telephone/Fax: 0191 581 0449
Therapist: Tony Attrill
Email: info@stopsmoking-uk.net
Website: www.allencarr.com

NORTHAMPTON
Telephone: 0800 0197 017
Therapists: Kim Bennett,
    Emma Sole
Email: kim@easywaybucks.co.uk
Website: www.allencarr.com

NORWICH
Telephone: 0800 389 2115
Therapists: David Piper and
    Gary Harris
Email: info@casyway
    norfolk.co.uk
Website: www.allencarr.com

NOTTINGHAM
Telephone: 0800 0197 017
Therapists: Kim Bennett,
    Emma Sole
Email: kim@easywaybucks.co.uk
Website: www.allencarr.com

OXFORD
Telephone: 0800 0197 017
Therapists: Kim Bennett,
    Emma Sole

Email: kim@easywaybucks.co.uk
Website: www.allencarr.com

PETERBOROUGH
Telephone: 0800 0197 017
Therapists: Kim Bennett,
    Emma Sole
Email: kim@easywaybucks.co.uk
Website: www.allencarr.com

PORTSMOUTH (OPENING SOON)
Telephone: 0800 389 2115
Website: www.allencarr.com

READING
Telephone: 0800 028 7257
Therapists: John Dicey,
    Colleen Dwyer, Sam Carroll,
    Emma Sole, James Pyper
Website: www.allencarr.com

SCOTLAND: GLASGOW AND
EDINBURGH
Telephone: 0131 449 7858
Therapists: Paul Melvin,
    Jim McCreadie
Email: info@easyway
    scotland.co.uk
Website: www.allencarr.com

SHEFFIELD
Telephone: 0800 804 6796
Therapist: Rob Groves
Email: stopsmoking@easyway
    yorkshire.co.uk
Website: www.allencarr.com

SHREWSBURY
Telephone: 01270 501 487
Therapist: Debbie Brewer-West
Email: debbie@easyway2stop
  smoking.co.uk
Website: www.allencarr.com

SOUTHAMPTON
Telephone: 0800 028 7257/01425
272 757
Therapists: John Dicey,
  Colleen Dwyer, Sam Carroll,
  Emma Sole, James Pyper
Email: easywayadmin@
  tiscali.co.uk
Website: www.allencarr.com

SOUTHPORT
Telephone: 0800 077 6187
Therapist: Mark Keen
mark@easywaylancashire.co.uk
Website: www.allencarr.com

STAINES/HEATHROW
Telephone: 0800 028 7257
Therapists: John Dicey,
  Colleen Dwyer, Sam Carroll,
  Emma Sole, James Pyper
Website: www.allencarr.com

STEVENAGE
Telephone: 0800 019 7017
Therapists: Kim Bennett,
  Emma Sole
Email: kim@easywaybucks.co.uk
Website: www.allencarr.com

STOKE
Telephone: 01270 501 487
Therapist: Debbie Brewer-West
Email: debbie@easyway2stop
  smoking.co.uk
Website: www.allencarr.com

SURREY
Telephone: 020 8944 7761
Fax: 020 8944 8619
Therapists: John Dicey, Sue
  Bolshaw, Sam Carroll, Colleen
  Dwyer, Crispin Hay, Jenny
  Rutherford, Emma Sole, Rob
  Fielding, James Pyper
Email: mail@allencarr.com
Website: www.allencarr.com

SWINDON
Tel: 0117 950 1441
Therapist: Charles Holdsworth
  Hunt
Email: stopsmoking@easyway
  bristol.co.uk
Website: www.allencarr.com

TELFORD
Telephone: 01270 501 487
Therapist: Debbie Brewer-West
Email: debbie@easyway2stop
  smoking.co.uk
Website: www.allencarr.com

WATFORD (OPENING SOON)
Telephone: 0800 389 2115
Website: www.allencarr.com

WORCESTER

Telephone: 0800 321 3007
Therapist: Rob Fielding
Website: www.allencarr.com

AUSTRALIA

NORTH QUEENSLAND

Telephone: 1300 85 1175
Therapist: Tara Pickard-Clark
Email: nqld@allencarr.com.au
Website: www.allencarr.com

SOUTH AUSTRALIA

Telephone: (08) 8341 0898
Therapist: Phillip Collins
Freecall: 1300 88 60 31
Email: sa@allencarr.com.au
Website: www.allencarr.com

SOUTH QUEENSLAND

Telephone: 1300 855 806
Therapist: Jonathan Wills
Email: sqld@allencarr.com.au
Website: www.allencarr.com

SYDNEY, NEW SOUTH WALES

Telephone/Fax: 1300 785180
Therapist: Natalie Clays
Email: nsw@allencarr.com.au
Website: www.allencarr.com

VICTORIA, TASMANIA, ACT

Telephone: 03 9894 8866
Freecall: 1300 790 565
Therapist: Gail Morris
Email: info@allencarr.com.au
Website: www.allencarr.com

WESTERN AUSTRALIA

Telephone: 1300 55 78 01
Therapist: Dianne Fisher
Email: wa@allencarr.com.au
Website: www.allencarr.com

AUSTRIA

SESSIONS HELD THROUGHOUT AUSTRIA

Free telephone for information
and booking: 0800RAUCHEN
(0800 7282436)
Telephone: 0043 (0)3512 44755
Therapist: Erich Kellermann and
team
Email: info@allen-carr.at
Website: www.allencarr.com

BELGIUM

ANTWERP

Telephone: 03 281 6255
Fax: 03 744 0608.
Therapist: Dirk Nielandt
Email: easyway@dirknielandt.be
Website: www.allencarr.com

BULGARIA

Telephone: 0800 14104
Therapist: Stoyan Tonev
Email: stoyan@easyway.bg
Website: www.allencarr.com

CANADA

Toll free: 1 866 666 4299/905
   8497736
Therapist: Damian O'Hara
Seminars held in Toronto and
   Vancouver
Corporate programs available
   throughout Canada
Email: info@theeasywaytostop
   smoking.com
Website: www.allencarr.com

CHILE

Therapist: Claudia Sarmiento
Email: contacto@allencarr.cl
Website: www.allencarr.com

COLOMBIA

BOGOTA
Telephone: (57 1) 245 6910
Therapist: Jose Manuel Duran
Email: easywaycolombia@
   cable.net.co
Website: www.allencarr.com

CYPRUS

Telephone: 0035 77 77 78 30
Therapist: Kyriacos Michaelides
Email: info@allencarr.com.cy
Website: www.allencarr.com

CZECH REPUBLIC

Telephone: 00420 774 568 748/
   00420 774 KOURIT
Therapist: Adriana Dubecka
Email: terapeut@allencarr.cz
Website: www.allencarr.com

DENMARK

SESSIONS HELD THROUGHOUT
   DENMARK
Telephone: 0045 70267711
Therapist: Mette Fonss
Email: mette@easyway.dk
Website: www.allencarr.com

ECUADOR

Telephone/Fax: 02 2820 920
Therapist: Ingrid Wittich
Email: toisan@pi.pro.ec
Website: www.allencarr.com

FRANCE

SESSIONS HELD THROUGHOUT
   FRANCE
Central booking line:
   0800FUMEUR (Freephone)
Telephone: 33 (4) 91 33 54 55
Therapists: Erick Serre and team
Email: info@allencarr.fr
Website: www.allencarr.com

GERMANY

Free telephone for information
and booking:
08000RAUCHEN (0800
07282436)
Telephone: 0049 (0) 8031
90190–0
Therapists: Erich Kellermann and
team
Email: info@allen-carr.de
Website: www.allencarr.com

GREECE

Telephone: 0030 210 5224087
Therapist: Panos Tzouras
Email: panos@allencarr.gr
Website: www.allencarr.com

ICELAND

REYKJAVIK
Telephone: 553 9590
Therapist: Petur Einarsson
Email: easyway@easyway.is
Website: www.allencarr.com

INDIA

BANGALORE AND CHENNAI
Therapist: Suresh Shottam
Website: www.allencarr.com

ISRAEL

Telephone: 03 5467771
Therapists: Ramy Romanovsky,
Aviv Leibovitz
Email: info@allencarr.co.il
Website: www.allencarr.com

ITALY

Telephone/Fax: 02 7060 2438
Therapist: Francesca Cesati
Email: info@easywayitalia.com
Website: www.allencarr.com

JAPAN

Telephone: 0081 3 3507 4020
Therapist: Miho Shimada
Email: info@allen-carr.jp
Website: www.allencarr.com

MAURITIUS

Telephone: 00230 727 5103
Therapist: Heidi Houreau
Email: allencarrmauritius@
yahoo.com
Website: www.allencarr.com

MEXICO

SESSIONS HELD THROUGHOUT
   MEXICO
Telephone: 052 55 2623 0631
Therapists: Jorge Davo and Mario
   Campuzano Otero
Email: info@allencarr-mexico.com
Website: www.allencarr.com

NETHERLANDS

AMSTERDAM
Telephone: 020 465 4665
Fax: 020 465 6682
Therapist: Eveline de Mooij
Email: amsterdam@allencarr.nl
Website: www.allencarr.com

NIJMEGEN
Telephone: 024 360 33 05
Therapist: Jacqueline van den
   Bosch
Email: nijmegen@allencarr.nl
Website: www.allencarr.com

ROTTERDAM
Telephone: 010 244 0709
Fax: 010 244 07 10
Therapist: Kitty van't Hof
Email: rotterdam@allencarr.nl
Website: www.allencarr.com

UTRECHT
Telephone: 035 602 94 58
Therapist: Paula Rooduijn
Email: soest@allencarr.nl
Website: www.allencarr.com

NEW ZEALAND

NORTH ISLAND — AUCKLAND
Telephone: 09 817 5396
Therapist: Vickie Macrae
Email: vickie@easywaynz.co.nz
Website: www.allencarr.com

SOUTH ISLAND —
   CHRISTCHURCH
Therapist: Laurence Cooke
Email: laurence@easyway
   southisland.co.nz
Website: www.allencarr.com

NORWAY

OSLO
Telephone: 23 27 29 39
Therapist: Laila Thorsen
Email: post@easyway-norge.no
Website: www.allencarr.com

POLAND

SESSIONS HELD THROUGHOUT
   POLAND
Telephone: 022 621 36 11
Therapist: Anna Kabat
Email: info@allen-carr.pl
Website: www.allencarr.com

PORTUGAL

OPORTO
Telephone: 22 9958698
Therapist: Ria Slof

Email: info@comodeixarde
fumar.com
Website: www.allencarr.com

REPUBLIC OF IRELAND

DUBLIN AND CORK
Lo-Call 1 890 ESYWAY (37 99 29)
Telephone: 01 499 9010 (4 lines)
Therapists: Brenda Sweeney and
team
Email: info@allencarr.ie
Website: www.allencarr.com

SERBIA

BELGRADE
Telephone: (0)11 308 8686
Therapist: Milos Rakovic
Email: office@allencarr.co.yu
or milos.rakovic@
allencarrserbia.com
Website: www.allencarr.com

SINGAPORE
(opening 2009)

Therapist: Pam Oei
Website: www.allencarr.com

SLOVAKIA

Telephone: 00421 908 572 551
Therapist: Adriana Dubecka
Email: terapeut@allencarr.sk
Website: www.allencarr.com

SOUTH AFRICA

Central Booking Line:
0861 100 200

HEAD OFFICE AND CAPE TOWN
CLINIC
Telephone: 021 851 5883
Mobile: 083 600 5555
Therapist: Dr Charles Nel
Email: easyway@allencarr.co.za
Website: www.allencarr.com

PRETORIA
Telephone: 084 (EASYWAY)
327 9929
Therapist: Dudley Garner
Email: info@allencarr.co.za
Website: www.allencarr.com

SPAIN

Website: www.allencarr.com

SWEDEN

GOTEBORG AND MALMÖ
Telephone: 031 24 01 00
Email: info@allencarr.nu
Website: www.allencarr.com

STOCKHOLM
Telephone: 08 5999 5731
Therapist: Nina Ljingquist
Email: info@allencarr.se
Website: www.allencarr.com

SWITZERLAND

SESSIONS HELD THROUGHOUT
SWITZERLAND

Free telephone for information
and booking: 0800RAUCHEN
(0800 7282436)
Telephone: 0041 (0)52 383 3773
Fax: 0041 (0)52 3833774
Therapists: Cyrill Argast and
team

SESSIONS SUISSE ROMAND AND
SVIZZERA ITALIA

Telephone: 0800 386 387
Email: info@allen-carr.ch
Website: www.allencarr.com

TURKEY

SESSIONS HELD THROUGHOUT
TURKEY

Telephone: 0090 212 358 5307
Therapist: Emre Ustunucar
Email: info@allencarrturkiye.com
Website: www.allencarr.com

USA

SESSIONS HELD THROUGHOUT
USA

Central information and bookings,
toll free: 1 866 666 4299
Therapist: Damian O'Hara
Email: info@theeasywaytostop
smoking.com
Website: www.allencarr.com
Seminars held regularly in
New York and Los Angeles
Corporate programs available
throughout the USA.

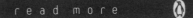

ALLEN CARR

If you enjoyed this book, there are several ways you can read more by the same author and make sure you get the inside track on all Penguin books.

Order any of the following titles direct:

0140244751   THE ONLY WAY TO STOP SMOKING PERMANENTLY   £9.99
'His greatest skill is in removing the psychological dependence' *Sunday Times*
'Allow Allen Carr to help you escape painlessly today' *Observer*

0140263586   ALLEN CARR'S EASYWEIGH TO LOSE WEIGHT   £8.99
Allen Carr applies his logical, common sense approach to food, suggesting
principles to follow that will lead to healthier eating, greater wellbeing and
permanent weight loss.

0140278370   THE EASYWAY TO ENJOY FLYING   £7.99
With his characteristic humour and pragmatism, Allen Carr demonstrates that
fear can be easily, successfully and permanently overcome as people understand
how safe flying really is.

0140289003   THE LITTLE BOOK OF QUITTING   £2.99
A perfect gift book and impulse purchase for those who want to give up or for
people eager to help smokers kick the habit.

Simply call Penguin c/o Bookpost on **01624 677237** and have your credit/debit card ready.
Alternatively e-mail your order to **bookshop@enterprise.net**. Postage and package is free
in mainland UK. Overseas customers must add £2 per book. Prices and availability subject
to change without notice.

*Visit www.penguin.com and find out first about forthcoming titles, read
exclusive material and author interviews, and enter exciting competitions.
You can also browse through thousands of Penguin books and buy online.*

IT'S NEVER BEEN EASIER TO READ MORE WITH PENGUIN

*Frustrated by the quality of books available at Exeter station for his journey back to
London one day in 1935, Allen Lane decided to do something about it. The Penguin
paperback was born that day, and with it first-class writing became available to a mass
audience for the very first time. This book is a direct descendant of those original
Penguins and Lane's momentous vision. What will you read next?*

ALLEN CARR'S EASY WAY TO STOP SMOKING

The Easy Way just got easier...

Now available as a Penguin Audiobook

Available from www.penguin.co.uk, all good bookshops and as a digital audiobook from www.audible.co.uk

live more